Intimate
Friendships

Dr. James Ramey is Director of the Center for the Study of Innovative Life Styles and Senior Research Associate at the Center for Policy Research in New York. He was formerly a Professor, Graduate School, Drexel University and Associate Dean, Pratt Institute. Dr. Ramey is a member of and has held national office in several professional societies. His current research includes ongoing studies of group marriage, complex living groups and intimate groups and networks. He has written several books and more than 60 professional articles, book chapters, and monographs.

Intimate Friendships

JAMES W. RAMEY

A SPECTRUM BOOK

PRENTICE-HALL, INC., Englewood Cliffs, New Jersey

Library of Congress Cataloging in Publication Data

Ramey, James W
  Intimate friendships.

  (A Spectrum book)
  Includes bibliographical references.
    1. Interpersonal relations.   2. Intimacy (Psychology)   3. Friendship.   I. Title.
  HM132.R25   301.11′2   75-28206
  ISBN 0-13-476903-1
  ISBN 0-13-476895-7 pbk.

A Spectrum Book

10   9   8   7   6   5   4   3   2   1

Printed in the United States of America

Prentice-Hall International, Inc., *London*
Prentice-Hall of Australia Pty. Ltd., *Sydney*
Prentice-Hall of Canada, Ltd., *Toronto*
Prentice-Hall of India Private Limited, *New Delhi*
Prentice-Hall of Japan, Inc., *Tokyo*
Prentice-Hall of Southeast Asia (Pte.) Ltd., *Singapore*

Contents

WITHDRAWN

Preface

Intimate friendships include any and all of the various kinds of relationships, primary or not (including monogamous marriage), that involve some degree of social, emotional, sexual, intellectual, family, or career intimacy, wherein interaction between persons is more important than, but may include, sexual relations. Intimate friendship involves an attitude toward sexuality that is applied to all of life—that sex is a part of living and an appropriate element in many other types of relating. One tests for its appropriateness in a given situation just as one tests any other element of living for appropriateness.

Previous books about marriage alternatives have concentrated on the couple because it is expected in our society that people will interact as couples—presenting a "couple-front" to the world, especially if they are married. The basic building block or unit in society is now the individual rather than the nuclear family because the individual can perform all the functions once associated with the family if s/he chooses to do so. It is therefore from the individual rather than the couple-front point of view that this book, based on current research, explores the spectrum of possible intimate relationships ranging from celibacy to group marriage. The focus is on the advantages and disadvantages of each lifestyle alternative, seen from the points of view both of the individual who is opting for a primary relationship and of the one who is not.

We are in the midst of a pluralistic revolution that is replacing the Freudian conceptualization of marriage, the family, and human sexuality and growth. The pluralistic model, which recognizes more than one life style as viable and acceptable, is a change model in which the constant in society is seen as change and conflict rather than as equilibrium. In interpersonal relationships, especially those involving a primary partner, the change model is a process-oriented growth model as opposed to the static traditional model; and a major function of this book is to help the reader understand why the difference is so important to maintaining growth in a relationship.

My thanks to the many residents in our ongoing studies of group marriage, complex living groups, and intimate groups and networks, who have spent long hours educating us to the facts of life, both problems and joys, as they are living them in lifestyles that are not "monogamous-nuclear-family." This book is dedicated to them as well as to my own primary partner, Betty, whose executive ear for the discordant note has kept me on target despite my tendency to wander off and examine interesting byways.

Intimate
Friendships

Why Is Marriage in Transition?

*College groups presume that parents and others of their parents'
generation are largely unaware of, much less involved in, any kind of
nonmonogamous lifestyle other than adultery. Sexual openness is considered
by many students to be a symbol of the new generation. Older adults feel just
the opposite to be the case. They claim that sexual activity outside marriage
is adult activity and deny that students do more than simply* talk-about *such
things. Parents, in particular, strive to hide their* own *activities from their
children and tend to deny the possibility that their children might be sexually
active.*

*A recent Cornell University study asked both parents and students if they
had ever known anybody who had cohabited (lived together without being
married). A third of the parents indicated that their own children had
cohabited, but two-thirds of those children reported that either they or their
siblings have cohabited. Almost sixty per cent of the parents knew someone of
their own generation who had cohabited, but only twenty per cent of their
children knew of such persons. Since two-thirds of the parents disapproved of
premarital sexual activity whereas two-thirds of the students thought it was
all right, it is understandable that most families are not likely to exchange
information or points of view in this highly charged area (See Macklin,
1974).*

Individuals of all ages want to know more about various lifestyle choices in order to make more intelligent decisions about their own lives and to have a clearer understanding of what others are doing and why. Do you have to be married to live happily ever after? A lot of people think so. Until recently, America was the most "married" nation in the world, and those who got divorced tended to remarry quickly. Today, fewer get married, more get divorced, and the unmarried and divorced portions of the population are rising rapidly.

Marriage has become a choice rather than an imperative. What is happening? No doubt you already have explored the various aspects of traditional marriage in considerable depth, perhaps in a classroom setting, but certainly through the process of growing up in this society. This assumption allows us to concentrate on exploring the many types of intimate friendship in the hope of insuring that the choices we make among various alternative lifestyles are made as rationally as possible.

What do we mean by intimate friendships? All the many types of relationships, including primary relationships, that involve some degree of social, sexual, emotional, intellectual, family, or career intimacy. These are relationships in which the interaction between persons is more important than, but may include, genital to genital interaction. This definition includes several types of marriage of course, as well as many other lifestyles.

1

Antecedents: Where Is Marriage Coming From?

This book is written from the point of view of the individual. Most books having to do with lifestyles tacitly assume a couple-front approach. There are several reasons for this, including the existence of two sexes (and as some would have you believe, two species); the fact that, until recently, most people in America got married; and the assumption that because it has always been this way, this is the way it will continue in the future. This last reason is part of the traditional view of society as a social system that maintains equilibrium by the self-correcting device we call consensus. In this view of society, as espoused by Parsons (1951) and others, any variation or change in society is an aberration that must and will be noted and corrected.

I do not buy this description of society. What is constant in life is change and conflict. Change and conflict continue until something happens, temporarily, to stop them (see Dahrendorf, 1958). This constant flux and motion in society is duplicated in organizations and in smaller groups, even in families, and one of the myths every child has to unlearn is the myth of stability in systems. Unfortunately, many of us never find out that it *is* a

3

myth, so we lead rather unhappy lives because something is always happening to destabilize things that concern us.

One reason for our confusion about how society functions is our tendency to subscribe to public images. Every society, organization, group, or family has a public image and a private image. The public image is the ritual or "ideal" prescribed behavior that is expressed in formal rules and laws. Hardly anyone ever lives up to these rules, although they may be evoked in times of crisis to chastise an individual or group that gets out of line. Many researchers have called attention to the great difference between the prescribed "ideal" behavior (the *ought*) and what people really do (the *is*). In 1953, Kinsey said: "The law is used for reasons that have nothing to do with the protection of individual rights, particularly in areas where legal codes bear upon lifestyle choices, intimacy patterns, sexual behaviors, and have more to do with assumptions about how people *ought* to act than about how they *actually* live." In 1970, John Cuber wrote: "In many ways, people function in two separate and often contradictory spheres. One consists of a set of proscriptions concerning what behavior *ought* to occur and *why* it should follow the outline proscribed. This is called the 'normative order.' The other consists of what people *actually* do in concrete instances when overt behavior is observed. The two are in direct conflict in most every aspect of sex, marriage and family life." Some anthropologists have even suggested that the norms serve the function of obscuring actual behavior, as for example, to please the missionaries from the Western Cultures (Harris, 1968). Changes in ideal norms always lag behind change in the values, attitudes, and actual behavior of people in a society, thus also making it very difficult to discover whether or not there has, in fact, been any change. (One handy index to the relative "lag" is the degree and manner in which legal regulations are enforced or ignored.)

Much of the confusion today about whether there has been any change in sexual behavior and attitudes stems from this confusion of the *is* and the *ought*. Since many writers tell us what they *think* is happening or *should be happening,* and even those who base their conclusions on research usually report what people *say* rather than what they *do*, it is easy to understand why so many professionals in the behavioral and biomedical fields are proclaiming fervently that nothing has changed since the Kinsey reports in 1948, or at the very most, that the only change has been an increase in premarital sexual experience among college women (see, for example, Udry, 1974). Such reports are hard to take seriously in view of the revolutionary changes that have occurred in contraception and abortion alone; but they are understandable if one assumes that the respondents answered survey questions in terms of normative behavior (or as they *should* behave) instead of reporting the unvarnished reality.

Since World War II, technological and biological changes have been so revolutionary that they have far outrun our ability to maintain a broad overview of how interpersonal relationships have also changed. There is a complex and inevitable balance between technology, biology and the way in which individuals, and ultimately society, function. We can see the women's rights movement as the opening round in a growing sexual revolution that is in the process of redressing that balance. It *is* a sexual revolution and not just a "gradual loosening up of the moral fabric," because the participants have redefined the "givens" in such a manner as to preclude their coexistence with the previous Freudian definition of these givens. This is what Kuhn (1962) calls a "paradigm change—one in which people define the same facts in totally different and incompatible ways." The last time it occurred with respect to sexuality was when the Freudian revolution overturned the Victorian concept of sexuality.

Since the biological and technological changes have already occurred, the changes in how people relate to each other and in sexuality are *effects*, not *causes* (Ramey, 1972a). Those who argue that "thus and so will occur because of the women's movement" or "because of premarital intimacy" are missing the point; and their "calls for action" to deal with these "social aberrations" are a bit like Don Quixote tilting at windmills.

Many people are of the opinion that alternate lifestyles are just another youthful fad and that as young people "grow up" and "accept responsibility" they will turn away from such youthful experiments and settle down into conventional marriages. Many social scientists of the traditional or fundamental schools agree. They do not see these alternatives as part of the sexual revolution; and they are apt to cite the existence of current types of alternate lifestyles as historically typical of bohemian or intellectual deviant subcultures. The commune, for example, has been a viable variant family form for at least 2,000 years, but has never involved more than a minute portion of the world's people.

As we shift from industrial to postindustrial society, and from scarcity to affluence, the work ethic is no longer sufficient; yet a leisure ethic is abhorrent and immoral in the eyes of most people. Understandably, they resist the suggestion that adulthood itself may have to be redefined in terms of values and attitudes currently associated with "unrealistic" youth—such as openness to experience, change, intimacy and trust, cultivation of personal growth, and exploration of "inner space." Indeed, these may be the very qualities necessary for lifelong survival in the new era.

But the givens *are* different today than they ever were before. Positive contraception is a fact, and so is abortion on demand. The female lifespan in 1900 was 48 years, and 18 of those years—from age 22–40—were devoted to maternity. In 1970 the female lifespan was 74 years, and ten years—from age 20–30—were devoted to maternity (See Sullerot, 1971); the average American woman today completes the family size she desires by age 26 (Udry, 1974). Nevertheless, Americans today are far from having as few children as they desire (See Ryder and Westoff, 1969); and the likelihood is that it will be some time before the desire and the reality merge. The important factor, however, is that the vast increase in nonmaternity years for women will have a marked effect on their worldview and on their lifestyles.

The psychological impact of the women's rights' movement has already permeated our society. Women are no longer content to "keep their places" and slowly but surely the socialization of females is shifting. Conventional women today have some very unconventional attitudes. They are all aware that women are paid less than men for the same jobs and they no longer feel that this is justifiable discrimination (Tavris and Jayaratne, 1973). The woman who assumes an occupational role through a desire for self-realization exerts an influence on her daughter's development in which the girl identifies with and incorporates many of her mother's ego characteristics (Douvan, 1963). These girls admire their mothers more, have a concept of the feminine role which includes a wide range of possibilities, develop a more clearly formed self-concept, and tend, in general, to become less "traditionally feminine" personalities (Nye and Hoffman, 1963). This is no doubt in part due to the shift in family power. A working wife participates more than the nonworking wife in making decisions about the family economy; and the higher her income, the more she is likely to share in such decision-making (Noordhoek and Smith, 1972). Fifty per cent of the wives in the nation work outside the home today; and although they currently receive only about 75 per cent as much salary as men doing comparable work, there is every reason to believe that the Equal Opportunity Act will gradually change this pattern. Furthermore, there is evidence that dual income couples expect *more* interaction and joint activity in their leisure time (Blood, 1963), and that they actually devote more direct time to their children than do nonworking wives. (In fact, a child may receive its nonworking mother's undivided attention no more than a half-hour or an hour a day (Skolnick, 1973).

Historically, we have been a nation on the move. As new immigrant waves came to the east coast, young people moved west, and each generation has shown increased mobility until today, one-fifth of the population moves at least as far as the next county every year. As a result of this mobility, kinship, neighborhood, and friendship ties no longer provide the social relationships we all seem to need. As Philip Slater (1968) indicated, the married couple or nuclear family is forced to take up the slack, and has shown marked inability to do so, with a resultant vast increase in divorce and unhappiness. Likewise there has been a shift in writing about marriage, with more and more stress on "companionate" rather than "traditional" or male dominant marriage. A companionate marriage is one in which companionship rather than childbearing is the major focus. Declaring that families should be more democratic doesn't make it so. However, so many people said it that soon a few went out into the field to check. Unfortunately, they tended to interview only one family member, usually either the mother or the father. Since these people spoke for their entire family, there was no independent check on their responses, and since people always "put their best foot forward," many of them reported that their marriages and/or families were truly democratic. Because nobody dared break the taboo about invading family privacy, there was little or no check on actual family behavior; and as Laing (1971) said: "Families practice mystification: they have complicated stratagems for keeping people in the dark about what is going on, and in the dark that they are in the dark." To complicate matters further, no very good definition of the family exists!

As Spiegel (1971) reported, "instead of finding a clearcut definition of the family easy to achieve, we discovered families exhibiting the most astonishing variance in their structure and function. Even those functions that were apparently universal, such as the socialization of children, the satisfaction of sexual needs, or the biological and material maintenance of members of the family, were carried out in such various ways with such different implications that it proved impossible to obtain meaningful patterns without reference to the surrounding social system." Unable to define the family clearly, some researchers have concentrated on the household, or living unit, instead (Ramey, 1973; Bohannan, 1963). As Bohannan points out, the household is a place where the functions usually ascribed to the family are performed.

Nevertheless, journalists, the general public, and many professionals in the field assume that the family is the nuclear family, that is, working father, housewife mother, and children. They seem unaware that this "ideal" family is far from being the majority pattern in America; so that by inference, most Americans live in "deviant" family forms, such as single parent families, dual-career families, extended families, childless couples, postchildrearing families, or are among the unmarried, widowed, divorced, separated, or "others" category (Ramey, 1972b).

Since the early 1960s, a distinct change has occurred in writing about the nuclear family. Based largely on such external evidence as student uprisings, drug addiction, teenage crime, skyrocketing divorce rates, sexual promiscuity, and the like, social scientists of the stature of Margaret Mead began to suggest that the nuclear family was in trouble, that it was inherently unstable because it was too small a unit to survive in today's world, and that it was perhaps on the way out (see Goode, 1963). Laslett (1973) argued that "the increase in family privacy in recent years may result in less social control over what goes on in families, as well as less social support for family roles, hence these increases in family strains that have led to dissatisfaction with the nuclear family."

The key issue may well be the inherent paradox in all interpersonal relationships, especially primary relationships—the tension between freedom and commitment. Legally, marriage is a contractual relationship in which the wife is the *dependent* and *subordinate* of the husband. He and she cannot legally change that relationship. A 1974 Roper poll indicated that 57 per cent of all women don't like being dependent and subordinate. For the first time, a majority of women indicated that they were in favor of efforts to strengthen women's position in society.

The "systems approach" only recently developed by psychologists and psychiatrists who set out to study the interaction of families with a schizophrenic member came up with the startling realization that the marital and family conflict in such families was not very different from that in families without schizophrenic members. In either case, they found that there are several factors present in every relationship. Whenever anyone communicates, his message either reinforces the ongoing definition of the relationship or suggests a shift of definition within the relationship. It is impossible not to communicate, *and the most important part of communication is nonverbal.* A central issue of communication is the reinforcement of either dominance or equality. The systems approach sees in any communication a person makes to another an attempt to control or define that relationship. The primary relationship, in these terms, is seen as a situation in which the couple must work out rules for living together as well as rules for making the rules. The couple need not necessarily be aware of the rules they are following, but they cannot, accordingly, avoid having them (Haley, 1963). A popular book on this theme was Berne's *Games People Play.*

Thus we see that the change and conflict conception of society does appear to be reflected in the family as well as in other relationships. The nonverbal aspect of this conflict is especially important. Most of us are not very adept at reading nonverbal communication, yet Henley (1974) indicates that the nonverbal message carries 4.3 times the weight of the verbal one. Nonverbal communication takes many forms, such as *demeanor* (women must sit in "ladylike" positions, but men can sit in undignified positions); *space* (the dominant person may not be approached as closely as the subordinate); and *touch* (the higher status person feels free to touch the lower status person, but not vice versa). *Eye contact* has been widely researched and Duncan (1969) says the most single important variable in eye contact is sex. Women watch men for visual cues, especially if they are in a primary relationship. Dominance is communicated by the stare. The averted glance signifies submission. As Henley (1974) indicates, although these nonverbal cues are involved in same-sex relationships as well as cross-sex relationships, it is in the male–female relationships that the power struggle is most evident; for when the female takes the dominant role by staring, touching, physical closeness, or loosening of demeanor, thus defying the norms governing male–female roles, men tend to deny the norm violation by substituting a different interpretation of the communication as being "sexual aggression!" Henley's short article, "Power, Sex, and Nonverbal Communication" is highly recommended reading.

Functionalists assume that social and sexual inequality must always be part of human society. For Parsons and Goode, social institutions like the family function to maintain social stability and consensus. But Moore (1958) sees that the family is already a part-time institution for most people, and that it is likely to become more so in the future. After all, as Mead (1968) pointed out, the modern nuclear self-contained family household was invented during the present century and confined generally to the United States, and we can expect that other variations in lifestyle will emerge with the same rapidity.

It is not unreasonable to suggest that we are caught up in a set of conflicting value systems, as these social scientists seem to be indicating. For one thing, we do not live in a monolithic society. What is true for the upper-middle class is not true for either the upper class or the lower class. But many sociologists think only in terms of what happens in the middle class, whereas most studies are done on working and lower class populations. In addition, different professionals interpret the same results from differing points of view, as we have mentioned earlier. Adding to the complexity of the situation is the "trickle-down" theory. According to this application of the diffusion of innovation, the innovators are usually upper-middle class individuals who are variously known as opinion leaders or innovators because others follow their lead. According to diffusion theory, when only 1 or 2 per cent do something, it doesn't "catch on"; but once 7 or 8 per cent diffusion occurs, the practice suddenly mushrooms. For example, before World War II, few women smoked cigarettes, although some had done so for thirty years. After the war, however, the practice increased at a very rapid rate because the critical point had finally been reached in the diffusion curve. Then the practice trickled down, from upper-middle class women to the nation at large. Similarly, the idea that it was all right for girls to wear jeans trickled down from the exclusive girl's colleges in the northeast. Higher education itself is another example of the diffusion process.

A number of alternative lifestyles have been imbedded in the upper-middle class for a long time. Most of these have been as well guarded from the public view as the inner workings of the nuclear family, and indeed, some of them have looked like conventional nuclear families. Social scientists have known that such alternate lifestyles existed but have assumed that they were unimportant "deviations" because they appeared to be very few in number. Even after the revelations of the Kinsey reports, little attention was paid to these lifestyles because the main focus of the Kinsey reports was on common sexual behaviors. Not until the early 1960s did attention begin to focus on consensual adultery and comarital sex (joint or couple-front sex outside the marriage); but once journalists and social scientists began to examine these practices, the spotlight soon began to broaden to encompass an ever-widening number of lifestyles.

At the same time, considerable attention was beginning to center on personal freedom, self-actualization, growth centers, encounter, and other manifestations of the single most important realization of the decade of the sixties—that the *individual, not the family,* is the basic building block of society. While the family was steadily losing importance as the locus of the primary functions that are necessary in any culture, such as work, reproduction, socialization and sexual activity, the individual steadily emerged as the arbiter of these necessary functions. In the affluent society, the individual can choose to maintain an independent household and carry out all of these functions alone. More important, a female individual can do so. What does this mean in practical terms?

It means that the female can negotiate on an equal footing with the male in the establishment of a primary relationship or any other kind of relationship. In the past, only females who were unusually gifted, or wealthy, or creative, or famous, or those who held high positions enjoyed this option. Today, growing numbers of young women are determined to opt for an equal position, and in view of their ability to control conception and earn a living independent of the male, many are succeeding.

That is why it is now possible to write this book, which will distinguish between those who cling to the old rules and those who espouse the new rules as well as explore the many ways in which people can be intimate friends under the new rules.

2

Complexity:
What Kinds of Relationships
Are Available Today?

Bart and George met while attending the Harvard Graduate School of Business. They roomed together during the course, and Bart was especially helpful to George, who was trying to get over the death of his wife, an experience which Bart likened in some ways to his own divorce several years earlier. One night Bart was awakened by the sounds of George crying in the next room, and he went in and comforted him physically, holding him in his arms while George worked through the crisis, during which George got an erection. Neither mentioned this, but the pair developed a deep friendship over the balance of their time in Cambridge.

Six months passed, during which they maintained touch by letter and phone. Then George stopped off in New York on his way to London and spent the night with Bart—a night that started with tentative, then intense, discussion of their mutual feelings, and wound up with the two in bed together. When George returned from London three days later, both had had time to think things over and they subsequently decided that they wanted to live together. Today, after fifteen years together, during which each has continued to have occasional heterosexual intimacy, they feel that their homosexual union is ideally suited to their needs. The relationship is also accepted by George's grown children.

This is but one of the many types of lifestyle choices we will examine and define in this chapter. It is typical of many relationships in one particular—it involves a primary relationship and occasional secondary relationships. What kinds of decisions are involved in determining relationship patterns?

We are basically problem-solving organisms, happiest when we are solving problems, and generally eager to progress to problems of ever-greater complexity. However, the process of perceiving the nature of reality problems, upon analysis, may require reevaluation of previous ideas and concepts and may also lead to the awareness that an irrational solution could lead to destructive consequences for self and others. We are all vulnerable to the imposition of authoritarian ritual solutions by society, especially when dealing with problems in taboo areas, such as departing from traditional and conventional lifestyle choices. Such so-called solutions actually block true solutions of problems. The fear of punishment imposed by authoritarian ritual diverts attention from cooperative exploration of mutual problems to solitary defensive rumination about how frightening the problems are and about what punishments conventional society may impose. If we think in the problem-solving frame of reference instead of accepting perceived ideas (dogma) *unevaluated,* the techniques for coping with differences in ideas can be developed creatively. Using differences as the basis for uncovering errors, we sift out sound statements of fact, so that free and sensitive communication focuses on searching out the truth about the nature of an objective reality problem (Denah Harris, 1960).

This is the process that has led to the reinterpretation of the "givens" about human sexuality and the nature of relationships and the meaning of life for those who espouse the cultivation of continuous growth, personal freedom, openness to experience and change, intimacy, and trust.

Alan Watts, in *Nature, Man and Woman,* said: "Sexuality is not a separate compartment of human life; it is a radiance pervading every human relationship, but assuming a particular intensity at certain points." Peterman (1972), as quoted by Francoeur (1974), laments that "experiences we would like to share with a close friend are often taboo because our friend happens to be of the same sex or of the opposite sex, of a different age, married or single, related or unrelated to us. Even though we are blessed with many friends, there are many times when society forbids these friends to really support and complement our needs. In the mirage of plenty, we starve." Which one is right? For many individuals Peterman is unquestionably on target; but for a growing minority, Watts plucks the more responsive chord. These individuals understand intimacy to include a potential sexual component as well as intellectual, social, and emotional components. Where is such a philosophy likely to lead?

In 1971 I completed a three-year study of people interested in examining the pros and cons of entering into group marriages or other types of complex living arrangements (Ramey, 1972c). Out of that initial study grew three longitudinal studies: one of group marriage, one of other types of complex living groups, and one of intimate friendship groups and networks. This last study came about because I found that many people in the initial study were involved in intimate groups or networks of friends (Ramey, 1975a). As a result of these ongoing studies, and especially the one on intimate groups and networks, I revised the paradigm I had previously suggested to explain the interrelationship of various alternate lifestyles on a rising scale of complexity that began with conventional monogamous marriage and ended with group marriage (Ramey, 1972a). The revision was called for by the realization that *individuals,* rather than couples, dictate the formation of various types of intimate friendships, an observation well documented by my own research and one that seems to fit the conclusions reached in the previous chapter rather well.

COMPLEXITY THEORY—THE AVAILABLE CHOICES

The individual has three basic choices available with respect to relating to others on an intimate friendship basis, which is to say entering into any type of intimate relationship. The *first* choice is to avoid any and all such relationships with others.

Although this option is rarely exercised, it is a viable option for some people. It is easier today than ever before to maintain one's own household, completely self-contained, relying on masturbation for sexual gratification. Readers who choose this option should obtain a copy of Betty Dodson's book, *Liberating Masturbation* (1974).

The *second* choice is to develop any or all of a variety of intimate relationships, *but no primary relationship.* These might include hetero-, homo-, or bisexual intimacy, during-college cohabitation, occasional intimacy with dates, swinging, having a lover, developing intimacy with friends, becoming part of an intimate group or network of friends, participating in a complex living arrangement that includes intimacy, such as living with a couple in a threesome, cohabiting with a roommate without developing a primary relationship, living with a group, or any combination of these activities. In this choice, as in the first, one can live alone in one's own household; and in either case it is now possible also to be a single parent if one wishes to have and/or raise a child. In the case of this second choice, it is also possible to live with others or another without establishing a primary relationship.

The *third* choice involves the decision to enter into a primary relationship. It involves two options. First, one can establish a monogamous primary relationship, such as a common law marriage, cohabitation with a primary partner, or a legal monogamous marriage. Even if the relationship is nominally monogamous, the probability is still very high that one or both partners will engage in nonconsensual adultery. Paul Gebhard, of the Institute of Sex Research, suggested in 1968 that cumulative incidence figures for extramarital intercourse by age 35 were about 60 per cent for the male and 40 per cent for the female (Gebhard, in Hunt, 1969). There is every reason to suspect that these percentages have increased since 1968. The second option includes all of the relationship choices available to the individual who develops a variety of intimate relationships but *without* establishing any primary relationships, *plus* the opportunity to enter into one of several types of primary relationship—such as a contract relationship, a trial marriage, a deliberately childfree relationship, or even a dual-primary relationship (group marriage).

In either option, the primary relationship may of course be heterosexual or homosexual, and may or may not involve legal marriage. In either option, also, the type of relationship one enters into may range from a traditional, dominant-submissive pair-bond to a relationship of peers, or a peer-bond. These are not either/or possibilities. The range from one to the other covers a host of variations on the theme; and for any one couple, there may be many shifts from one part of the scale to another over time.

LIFESTYLE DEFINITIONS

Celibacy.   The commonly accepted meaning of celibacy is to refrain from sexual activity, including all variations, even masturbation. ~~Intimate Friendships, James Ramey.~~

Uncommitted Dating.   Occasional sexual intimacy without legal or other commitment of any kind. Such a relationship may be very loving and giving and involved without implying any kind of long-term understanding.

Intimate Groups and Networks.   Individuals develop varying levels of intimacy in their various friendships, not only on the social, emotional, sexual, and intellectual levels, but often on family and business levels as well. Whether the individual is a partner in a primary relationship that espouses sexually open marriage or is not involved in any primary relationship, over time, he or she will begin to develop a circle of friends with similar lifestyle philosophies, and the likelihood is that sexual intimacy will develop between a number of individuals in such a group. As people move from place to place, these groups tend to become linked into intimate networks, especially over the long term. Individuals in such groups often develop primary relationships (which may include legal marriage) and sometimes develop complex living groups or group marriages. In a recent study (Ramey, 1975a) of 380 individuals in intimate groups or networks, 255 were married, 125 were single, and 54 of the singles were currently in primary relationships. Fifty per cent of the respondents were straight, 42 per cent were bisexual, and 6 per cent were gay (2 per cent weren't telling).

   Having a Lover.   Some intimate friends are very special; and relationships between such special friends may take on many of the attributes of a primary relationship without becoming as involved as would be the case in a "living-together" situation. Both individuals may be single, or one or both may be married. The relationship may be short- or long-term.

   Cohabitation.   Living together in an intimate relationship that may or may not include sexual intimacy and may or may not involve a primary commitment. It is not uncommon for one to progress from "playing the field" to having a lover, to cohabitation. Macklin (1974) indicates that about a third of all college students are cohabiting at any one time and that 70–90 per cent will cohabit before they graduate. Often the word "premarital" is used as a modifier for cohabitation. This is a holdover from the previous generation which liked to indulge in wishful thinking—the theory being that any one who cohabited was "trying out marriage" and would soon be taking out a marriage license (see Whitehurst, 1974). Actually, cohabitation without any expectation of necessary marriage has been a way of life for many lower class Americans for generations. Similarly, on the college campus, the odds are very low that one will marry the person with whom one cohabits. Finally, a growing number of postcollege middle class Americans are cohabiting, rather than getting married. In one circle of friends known to the author, involving

33 individuals, there are six married couples and four cohabiting couples (one lesbian) and the rest are singles. The average age in this network is 32.

Trial Marriage.   Cohabiting with a primary relationship partner with the explicit intent to decide whether or not to make the arrangement a permanent primary relationship, legal or otherwise.

Common Law Marriage.   Although the criteria for common law marriage vary somewhat from state to state, cohabitors in those states that do recognize common law marriage (Alabama, Colorado, Georgia, Idaho, Iowa, Kansas, Montana, Ohio, Oklahoma, Pennsylvania, Rhode Island, South Carolina, Texas, Washington, D.C., and the Virgin Islands) may, if they are not careful, find themselves considered legally married. The most common four criteria, or elements of common law marriage, are these: The male and female must agree to marry, they must cohabit, describe themselves as married, and be regarded in the community as married. For legal purposes, unmarried cohabitors must claim to be unmarried if they wish to remain that way. The court will look for evidence of a married state in case of a legal dispute, such as taking a trip together as husband and wife to get a cheaper airline fare, filing a joint tax return, or registering as man and wife at a motel.

Traditionally Monogamous Marriage.   A legal, heterosexual, sexually exclusive two-person relationship in which both participants and nonparticipants consider the couple married.

Contract Marriage.   A marriage in which the couple has agreed to contractual terms in addition to those imposed by law. Current legal opinion suggests that the court would enforce any contract provision except one that contravened the welfare of children of the marriage. Prenuptial contract agreements were once very common but have not been used much in recent times except in cases where considerable wealth is involved. It is difficult to evaluate the effectiveness of marriage contracts because few have been tested in court, and there is no way to ascertain the validity of a legal document until a court rules on it (see Sussman and Gold, 1974).

Voluntarily Childfree Marriage.   A growing number of couples are turning to childfree marriage as a way of giving the wife an equal opportunity to enjoy equality in the relationship. These couples recognize that the world of work is so organized today that it is extremely difficult for a mother to continue to compete in her career on an equal basis, especially after the birth of a second child; that children completely change the nature of the husband-wife relationship; and that a mother's options will be seriously narrowed for about twenty years. A 1973 study by the Institute of Life Insurance showed that 75 per cent of a national sample agreed that deliberate childlessness was "perfectly all right." Some couples put off having children without actually deciding to be a childfree couple except temporarily, until the wife finishes college and gets her career started. By that time she may be past the age (28) after which extremely few American women start families today. Such a couple, therefore, may wind up among the voluntarily childfree couples without ever having deliberately decided never to have children (see Veevers, 1973).

Homosexual Marriage.   Same-sex unions, while not legally binding, may be solemnized in religious ceremonies in some instances, and there is reason to believe that in California and in several other states, such a marriage actually may ultimately be declared legal because the law in those states does not specify that husband and wife must be of different sexes as long as a minister performs the ceremony. Many same-sex unions exist, both male–male and female–female, and a number have lasted for many years.

Trial marriage, common law marriage, contract marriage, childfree marriage, homosexual marriage, and traditional marriage are all *assumed* to be monogamous. Each of these relationships may be entered into without becoming legally married, that is, on a cohabiting basis. Each is assumed to involve a primary relationship.

Three types of extramarital relationships are common to many so-called monogamous marriages.

Nonconsensual Adultery. The practice of adultery without the consent of one's primary relationship partner.

Consensual Adultery. Adultery with the full knowledge and consent of one's primary relationship partner.

Swinging, or Comarital Sex. Swinging may involve two or more pair-bonded couples who mutually decide to switch sexual partners or engage in group sex. Swinging may also involve couples and singles in either triadic or larger group sexual encounters. Often the singles form pairs for the purpose of swinging.

The line is hard to draw between consensual and nonconsensual adultery because the agreement is often tacit and unspoken or there may be an agreement to do it but keep quiet about it. The Kinsey studies (1948, 1953) found the incidence of adultery on a cumulative basis by age 45 to include nearly 50 per cent of the husbands and 26 per cent of the wives. By 1968 this percentage had risen to 60 per cent for males and 40 per cent for females (Gebhard, in Hunt, 1969). As Cuber and Harroff (1966) reported, a majority of their upper-middle class sample "ignored the monogamous prescriptions about sex. While holding the marriage bond to be inviolable, they condoned extramarital sexual relationships. Some did so quite openly, but most practiced more or less effective concealment and observed various conventional pretenses." This approach appears to extend to swinging as well. Most swingers do not make an issue of their lifestyle. On the other hand, many swingers restrict their social contacts, by and large, to other swingers, so that their lifestyle is less likely to be questioned by others.

Three types of marriage remain to be defined. They differ significantly from those previously discussed in that they do not pretend to be monogamous.

Peer Marriage.   A partnership, the purpose of which is to permit and promote the growth of each partner and of the partnership itself, built around an ongoing dialogue to which each partner brings input from all unshared areas of experience. Implicit within such a relationship is the understanding that there will be no secrets and that all input—social, sexual, or career—will be considered legitimate. Peer relationships are epitomized by the Francoeurs' definition of "cool sex" as "egalitarian, single-standard, sensually diffused, and oriented toward intimacy and open relations with persons" (R. T. and A. K. Francoeur, 1973).

Sexually Open Marriage.   A marriage in which the partners agree to retain their sexual freedom on an individual, not a couple-front basis. Such an agreement may be found in any type of marriage, but it is most frequently found in those instances in which the marriage partners are striving toward or have already developed a peer marriage (see Knapp, 1975).

Group Marriage.   Each of the three or more participants in a group marriage has a primary relationship with at least two others in the group. The significant factor is the ability to sustain multiple primary relationships. My research suggests that the most common form of group marriage is the triad, a threesome in which each individual has a primary relationship with each of the other two, for a total of three primary relationships, as contrasted to none, one, or two primary relationships in a trio or threesome. The second most common group marriage format involves two couples (these were the most common of all in the Constantines' study, 1973).

Polygamous Groups, or Threesomes.   Trios come in several varieties. Some are bisexual, some are homosexual, some are heterosexual. In any case there are usually two partners of one sex and one of the other. As in all three-person groups, one person usually dominates the group. The others relate to the dominant person more than to each other, or else form a coalition against the third party (see Caplow, 1968). In the most common heterosexual format, the male–female relationships are strong and the same-sex relationship is weak. The two strong relationships may be primary relationships; and if so, assuming the dominant person is male, the group is polygamous, whereas if the dominant single is a female, the marriage is considered polyandrous. A frequent variation on this theme is the married couple with a live-in straight, homosexual, or bisexual lover who is clearly not part of the primary relationship. The lover, if bisexual, is expected to relate sexually to both partners, and either alone or in concert with the marriage partners regardless of sexual orientation.

Complex Living Groups.   When individuals agree to make life commitments as members of one particular group rather than through many different groups, they may constitute a commune, an "expanded family," a co-op, or some other type of complex living group. Although the number of common commitments will vary from group to group, the critical number is reached when the group sees itself as a group, rather than when the group reaches some absolute number. Complex living groups may involve no primary relationships or may include a mixture of primary and nonprimary relationships. They may also involve any of a variety of intimacy patterns ranging from celibacy to group marriage.

Pete and Sharon became roommates when Pete answered Sharon's ad for a "roomie" in which she forgot to indicate that she was looking for a female. He was so funny when she told him about the mistake that she agreed to have dinner with him and listen to his pitch, although she had no intention of rooming with a man. The dinner turned out to be one he prepared himself and Sharon had to admit that he cooked as well as she did. Somehow or other, as each talked about the problems they had had with previous roommates, the conviction grew between them that it would be very funny to room together and watch all the hilarious things that might occur as each brought home dates and as each provided the other with insights into how the other half of the human race functions.

Although things started off on a very tentative basis, soon Sharon and Pete were sharing things neither had ever been able to discuss with a member of the opposite sex before. They found that they actually were helpful to one another in evaluating dates and in breaking barriers to relating. Soon they became good friends, and they were able to talk about what each wanted from a permanent relationship. When Sharon got married after fifteen months of rooming with Pete, her new bridegroom, Harry, insisted that Pete be his best man, since Pete had helped Harry and Sharon work out their relationship problems and write a marriage contract. They remained close friends for as long as Pete stayed in the same state. Harry told Sharon many times that it was all right with him if she went to bed with Pete, something she hadn't done during the fifteen months they lived together. It was not until Pete moved to Cleveland, however, that she seriously considered sleeping with him, and finally did, after the three of them discussed it by long-distance telephone first.

COMPLEXITY THEORY: RELATING LEVEL OF CHOICE TO DEGREE OF COMPLEXITY

After discussing the available choices and briefly defining

these many choices, the question arises, how are they related to complexity? For some individuals, just sorting through all the available options may be a more complex problem than they wish to face. In the foreseeable future there will be even more choices available, but they will all fit into the degree of complexity scale which concerns us here. It should be obvious that any two-person relationship is more complex and involved than going it alone, although the experience of some people who have been married and then find themselves unmarried again (divorced, separated or widowed) is that singlehood is pretty hard to take after having gotten used to a two-person relationship. Those who have cohabited often express similar views.

We are gregarious creatures, and we do enjoy companionship. Nevertheless, the more persons involved, the more complex the relationships, especially if some of the relationships are primary relationships. Between two persons there can only be one relationship, but between three persons there are three direct relationships plus a number of coalition possibilities. The progression quickly becomes staggering. Each time you add one individual to the group you add the previous number of relationships plus the previous number of people in the group, thus:

Persons	2	3	4	5	6	7	8	9	10	11	12	13	14	15
Relationships	1	3	6	10	15	21	28	36	45	55	66	78	91	105

Very few individuals can find the time and energy to sustain a large number of relationships. We are much more likely to develop a few close relationships or a lot of shallow relationships than to develop a great many close relationships. In fact, many people develop only one primary relationship at a time. This may be a cross-sex or same sex relationship with an older or younger person who may be a close relative, friend, or lover. A primary relationship requires almost constant availability because it becomes central to the way one's life is organized. If one marries the other person in each primary relationship, we call the result *serial monogamy*. The average marriage that ends in divorce in the United States lasts less than seven years. Thus it is not uncommon to meet people who have been married several times; and as Etzioni (1974) remarked, "the prevalent form of marriage seems to be sequential monogamy, with the sequences growing ever shorter and the monogamy ever less monogamous."

It should be evident from this discussion of definitions that fewer and fewer individuals are likely to be involved in a particular type of relationship as the complexity of maintaining that particular lifestyle increases. Cohabiting with someone is more difficult than simply sharing an apartment with a room-mate. In the case of Sharon and Harry's marriage, it was much easier for Sharon to actually go to bed with Pete once Pete no longer lived in the same town, because that made it much less complicated. But suppose Pete had moved in with Sharon and Harry. That would have increased the complexity to a much greater degree than if she *had* maintained an intimate friend relationship with him, but he continued to live across town. Thus we can expect the following to hold true: The vast majority of individuals will live in two-person primary relationships. A smaller group will live alone, or in nonprimary relationships. Much smaller percentages will live in three-person or larger groups. But most of these individuals will also be involved in intimacy of other types from time to time (see Cogswell and Sussman, 1972).

3

Commitment: What Brings People Together and Why?

A New York management recruiting firm routinely poses the following stress question to job prospects. "Your wife and your child have both fallen into the river. Neither can swim and you only have time to rescue one of them. Which one will you save? Ninety-nine per cent answer, 'my wife.'" This illustrates male–female bonding.

According to some authorities, mother–child and male–female bonding are biological processes, although they do not always occur. "We tried to stop her, but she rushed right back into the burning building shouting that her baby was in there." This is mother–child bonding. Lionel Tiger (1970) argues that male–male bonding also occurs and that it is also a biologically based process that has to do with aggression and dominance. (The three musketeers were "one for all and all for one," for example.) In previous writing I have sought to make clear, by using the term pair-bond to encompass all such relationships, that any primary relationship has the same functions and problems as a marriage relationship. It is not my intent, however, to suggest a biological basis for primary relationships or other relationships by using this term. Specifically, I am inclined to agree with

Tiger, Fox (1971), and others who have suggested that often bonding has more to do with dominance than with caring. I have contrasted the pair-bond, which is generally a dominant-submissive relationship, with what I would call a peer-bond, *a union of equals, in which each is willing to assume unlimited liability for the other* (Ramey 1972c). In the previous chapter we considered the differing degree of complexity in various types of relationships. In this chapter we will discuss those lifestyles in terms of depth and complexity of commitment.

The process of becoming committed is a process of becoming involved, or investing one's self. While there may be some residual biological urges involved, today they are very weak indeed. We must look to other sources for the origins of commitment—of progressively limiting one's options with respect to other potential commitments as one invests more and more of one's energy in the development of one particular commitment. Varying degrees of commitment are involved in each of the lifestyles one might choose. Some are downright antithetical. For example, complex living groups, such as communes, enjoy a much greater chance of success if primary relationships are not allowed to form, or, if, when they do exist, they are broken up. Strong primary relationships drain off energy and involvement from the group. Consequently, successful groups have developed highly structured ways of breaking up primary relationships in favor of sharing with the group as a whole. They have promoted group-wide intimacy either by remaining celibate or by practicing some form of total sexual access to all members. In either case, interpersonal relationships have been closely regulated and institutionalized, and sexual access has not meant loose or promiscuous intimacy. In the next chapter, we will examine this problem of power versus peerdom in depth.

A committed relationship is one involving dialogue (an on-going, problem-solving, learning interaction process), trust, and responsibility. What factors are involved in developing commitment? The basic ingredient is opportunity, and opportunity depends on propinquity, that is, on two or more persons being in the same place at the same time. But proximity alone is not enough, in every case, to develop a relationship. Facing a common problem; sharing common background in terms of profession, social class, age, religion, ethnic origin, education, and residence; and achieving success in a joint endeavor are all likely to enhance the probability of developing commitment.

There are a number of theories about *why*, when all the situational factors are present that might be expected to result in such an outcome, we sometimes establish relationships and why, at other times, we do not. Some therapists feel that we develop either security-seeking or satisfaction-seeking relationships and that we do so only when we feel those needs (see Sullivan, 1947). Others would argue that relationships are imposed on people by the social structure and situation, or that relationships are simply established for practical reasons. Finally, many argue that there is a distinct difference between close "mediating groups" or primary groups in which face-to-face contact builds warmth and commitment and secondary relationships that are not emotionally important but merely serve functional purposes, such as babysitting, getting the plumbing fixed, or collecting for the Red Cross.

An examination of a number of actual relationships of various sorts suggests, however, that there are varying degrees of intimacy in different relationships with respect to six components of intimacy: intellectual, emotional, sexual, social, family, and work—and that the degree of commitment depends on the amount of caring and sharing involved in the relationship. Because time and energy are limited, we tend to invest both where we have the greatest involvement. An individual with no primary relationships might well have a number of social commitments that provide companionship—commitments within which he may share ideas, attitudes, and norms, and develop a backlog of shared experiences. Such a network of friends can be expected to generate both events that can be shared and general social activities. If some of the friends become intimate friends, it is likely that those particular friends will begin to take up a greater portion of the individual's time and energy. If sexual intimacy is also involved, the possibility then exists that one of these intimate relationships might become a primary relationship. Some individuals go to great lengths to avoid letting this happen. They may try to divide their time between several people or to share different types of activity with different people in an attempt to avoid "getting serious" with any particular one.

For most people there seems to be real effort required to overcome the socialization they have received from babyhood toward forming a primary relationship; usually, there is strong pressure from family, friends, and even from employers, to "get married." In this era when people leave home and often move great distances away, it is easier to avoid these pressures than it has been in the past, so that today, 12.6 million Americans are living alone and the number of single parent families is growing at three times the rate of two parent family growth (Etzioni, 1974). Nevertheless, most people do form primary relationships, at least for short periods of time.

Once formed, a primary relationship is not a static affair. It either grows or it withers. If it grows, it does so because the partners are investing time and energy in exploring, developing and consolidating their relationship rather than expending their energy and time on other things or people. Thus, when individuals who are part of an intimate group or network develop a primary relationship, they often either drop out of their former group or greatly reduce their sexual involvement with other friends while concentrating on developing the primary relationship. If they do not do this, they run the risk of developing a competing relationship with someone else. On the other hand, if they develop the primary relationship for a while, and how long depends on the people—it could be six months or three years—and then resume other sexually intimate relationships, the primary relationship will be less likely to be jeopardized by the ancillary relationships. It will have a head start on them and will, in addition, continue to grow faster than the other relationships possibly could, because the primary relationship partners can be expected to see to it that their other relationships are not allowed to impinge on the time or psychic space of the primary relationship.

Some individuals seem to turn their backs completely on all other sexually intimate relationships when they form a primary relationship, especially if it involves marriage. Why? For the men, the reasoning is traditional. They all expect to play around until they get married; but then they expect to marry women who will be theirs alone, as though they were buying shoes. For their wives this is a double bind. They were expected to be "liberated" before marriage, that is, they were supposed to be sexually active, like the men. But once married, they find that hubby doesn't want them to play the game anymore. It is still all right for him to "play around," of course. That is the male prerogative. But she is supposed to cut out the liberated nonsense and "be a good wife." This attitude on the part of the husband is more likely to lead to trouble today than in the past. In California there are now three divorces for every two marriages (Colton, 1974); and many wives rebel at some point early in the marriage and call for a redefinition of terms, "or else." Thus many marriages seem to be evolving into sexually open marriages sometime between the third and the tenth year (Knapp, 1974).

Weiss (1974) says that everybody needs to satisfy two types of need in order to live comfortably. He conjectures that "an adequate life organization needs a sense of attachment from which one gains a sense of at-homeness and security and without which one senses the loneliness of emotional isolation." This sense of attachment is a generalized feeling that one derives, usually, from a primary relationship. On the other hand, one needs the kind of social integration of which we spoke earlier—the friends who supply occasional reassurance of worth, or guidance, or shared interests and activities—for without this element in life, one suffers the loneliness of social isolation.

Some people are quite willing to enter into a primary relationship, while others are not so sure they are "willing to accept unlimited liability for a partner." For those individuals, there are other alternatives—various types of complex living groups—that still provide a center around which to organize their lives in a manner that will preclude both emotional and social isolation.

If the individual chooses this type of alternative then his commitment will be to a group rather than to an individual. Such a group demands three types of commitment response from members because group survival depends on dealing with three critical problems—continuance, cohesion, and control. As Kanter (1972) analyzes the problem, a group, in order to be successful, "must figure out how to get the work done, but without coercion; ensure that decisions are made, but to everyone's satisfaction; build close, fulfilling relationships, but without exclusiveness; choose and socialize new members; provide room for individual autonomy and uniqueness; and ensure agreement and shared perception of community process and values. A person is committed to a group or to a relationship when he himself is fully invested in it, so that the maintenance of his own internal being requires behavior that supports the social order." This identification of self with the group is what Cooley (1962) considers essential for self-realization.

In a group in which the individual has no primary relationship, these questions must be constantly addressed: Is the group making sufficient progress toward its goals to justify my continuing to invest energy in it that could be directed elsewhere? Furthermore, are the perceived aims and goals of the group still worthy of my continued support? Both types of commitment have long since been institutionalized for two-person marriage. Our society has made the decision that marriage meets these qualifications for commitment; but many individuals today are no longer certain that it does, at least, not without some serious modifications.

It is evident that complex living groups of the type Kanter is speaking about demand more than group maintenance and commitment to defined goals, however. The question of emotional attachment to the group is of equal importance. Members must feel emotionally bound to each other and to the group as a whole and be willing to "stick together," as Kanter puts it. This kind of affective commitment is often expressed in terms of people having come closer as a result of having survived difficulties together, of having "weathered the storm."

Again, we have described a type of commitment that is at the heart of a primary relationship. Thus it should be apparent that joining a complex living group is analogous to marrying a whole group instead of an individual. This is exactly why so many complex living groups fail. It is extremely difficult, especially today, to develop a group that can sustain this kind of commitment and cohesion in spite of the pull of the outer society. This is particularly true if the complex group is not a self-sustaining community with sharply defined boundaries between it and the larger society and one with little need for members to cross those boundaries. A complex group that depends on support through its members working "outside," for example, has a much greater problem with "boundary maintenance" than one that is internally self-supporting. Consequently we have been careful to use the term "complex living groups" rather than commune, or co-op, or intentional community, because there are many shades of difference in the organization of such complex groups and the differences can be most easily understood in terms of the degree of commitment required from their members.

Two special cases need to be examined in greater detail: threesomes and group marriages. We have defined two types of threesome. One involves living with a couple—presuming either that a primary relationship exists between the couple or that two members of the threesome have a primary relationship with the third but not with each other. The second type of threesome is a three person group marriage. In the latter case, each person would have a primary relationship with each of the other two. An individual who joins an existing primary relationship couple to form a threesome with no intention of forming a primary relationship with either of them may be able to satisfy both the social and attachment needs we spoke of earlier. Many people take this step for this reason, but some find that they then suffer increased emotional loneliness rather than less. Even though they may be fully accepted as members of the household, the presence of the special bond of "willingness to accept unlimited liability for the primary relationship partner" between the primary relationship partners makes the third person an outsider. In some cases individuals have gotten together as a threesome without *any* primary relationship ties and have avoided this problem. However, in each case, as growing together occurs, the ties either become stronger or the threesome breaks up. Typically, additional primary relationships develop. If the group consists of two persons of the same sex, and one of the other, the primary relationships are probably more likely to form on a cross-sex basis first if the single person is a female and in either direction if the single person is a male. If the threesome survives with two primary relationships, then a third one may ultimately form between the remaining two individuals, regardless of whether they are male or female; but this relationship is somewhat more likely to form between females than between males.

Threesomes are easier to form than any other kind of group larger than two. It is much easier for two people to agree on their mutual attraction to one other individual than to another couple or a larger group. The same goes for three individuals who are initially attracted to one another before any primary relationships have formed between them. A threesome also appears to be the most stable type of multiple live-in relationship. Many of the group marriages identified to date have been three person group marriages, and they have been equally distributed between one male–two female and one female–two male groups (Constantine and Constantine, 1973).

Although moving in with a couple may at first seem to be a way of avoiding getting into a primary relationship, the strong possibility exists that taking this step may ultimately lead one into an even more complex relationship than simply getting married. There is reason to believe, however, that relationships are easier to sustain in a group marriage of any size than in other types of complex living arrangements. For one thing, group marriages are extremely unlikely to have more than seven members, for even in a seven person marriage there are twenty-one potential primary relationships—six for each member—and it is unlikely that many people could develop and sustain six primary relationships simultaneously. Besides, a group of eight is unusually unstable, and susceptible to breaking up into two groups of four each.

Research on small groups has shown that a group of four members experiences less distance between the most dominant member and the rest of the group than groups of other sizes. The distance is somewhat greater in a group of three or five, greater still in a group of two and progressively greater in groups of six, seven, eight, nine, and so on. This is why groups of four or three predominate in group marriages. Groups of three may have an edge because the problems engendered by lack of symmetry force a trio to talk through their relationship in much greater detail than a group of four, which is usually composed of two couples, each of which has its own primary relationship to fall back on.

Precisely because the group marriage is seen by its participants as a set of multiple primary relationships, the degree of commitment to the group is likely to be much stronger from the outset than to a large complex group, particularly if, as is likely, that complex group seeks to break up primary relationships and avoid the formation of new ones. If the complex group does *not* make such demands, then it is likely to be a very loosely knit, amorphous group anyway; and therefore the potential member is even less likely to make the kind of all-out commitment to it that one would expect to make to a primary relationship. It should be noted, by the way, that it is not necessary that all the *possible* primary relationships in a group marriage be developed at the beginning, just as long as each member has at least two, since it *is* necessary for all the participants to be assured that each of them is capable of at least two simultaneous primary relationships. In a large group marriage it may take a number of years to develop all potential primary relationships; and indeed, this may never happen, particularly between some of the males.

Individuals in peer or sexually open primary relationships who form sexually intimate friendships often find, over time, that they are part of an intimate group or network of couples and singles that includes three types of members: core members, associated members, and affiliated members. *Core members* may be defined as those who have been sexually intimate with several other members in the group. In some groups this means heterosexual contact but does not necessarily mean bisexual or homosexual contact. *Associated members* are those who have been sexually intimate with at least two members of the group or network, one of whom may be his/her primary partner, either same-sexually or cross-sexually. *Affiliated members* are those who subscribe to group philosophy and are identified as members by others in the group although they are not currently involved sexually except with their primary partner, who is a core or associated member (Ramey, 1975a).

Such an intimate group or network involves the same three types of commitment demanded by the complex living group or group marriage, but in a significantly different configuration. The key factor is, of course, that the members do not share living quarters. Thus, even though the members may represent diverse individual characteristics, they share the common commitment to sexually open marriage philosophy, and they are very aware of who is in the group and who is not in the group. The area of divergence is with respect to the primary relationship. While some individual members may feel a diffuse emotional commitment to the group as a whole, others—both married and single—who are in primary relationships (or multiple primary relationships), share a more attenuated but still very important emotional commitment with the group or network. Because members do not share living quarters, they can regulate their degree of involvement to a much greater degree than is possible in a "living together" situation. In effect, they can participate to a greater or lesser degree, depending upon what is happening in other areas of their lives. Actually, intimate groups that have been in existence for many years seem to build more and more connective tissue with the passage of time. It is for this reason that we measure their degree of intimacy on six levels—social, intellectual, sexual, emotional, *family,* and *work*—for we find even stronger career and family ties in actual intimate groups than

Stoller postulated in his discussion of intimate networks of families in 1970. Intimate group members do many things together, ranging from foreign travel to putting business deals together, and from exchanging family members (children) to building a retirement farm or summer cabin together.

Ann left Ohio State University in the middle of her senior year to join a rural commune in upstate New York. Her initial impression of the group was based on reports from Roy, who had lived there during the summer of 1964, and on a couple of Newsletters put out by the group. She decided to join the group after reading about the great things they were doing and about their call for additional members in the *Modern Utopian* magazine. When she arrived, she found that because many members had left with the onset of cold weather she received a particularly warm welcome. She soon found, however, that the five women in the group were doing the lion's share of the work, aside from gathering firewood, while the nine men sat around the fire and rapped about how great it was to be a family, living free from the plastic society. She also discovered that three of the women were essentially monogamous, that is, two had monogamous primary relationships and the third had formed a monogamous trio with two of the men. Apparently, too, Ann was expected to sleep with any of the other five men who wanted to sleep with her.

Ann had grown up in an upper-middle class family in which the housekeeper did the chores, from cooking and shopping to cleaning and washing; and her enthusiasm for communal life quickly waned as the weeks rolled by. When she began "consciousness raising" with the other women in the group, she found, to her amazement, that they resented her efforts even more than the men, who just ignored or poked fun at her efforts. Early in the spring she left the group and moved to New York City, where she was able to work out an arrangement at City College that allowed her to make up the time she had lost in school, transfer her credits, and graduate at the same time she would have graduated had she stayed at Ohio State.

Shortly after getting a job in a publishing house, Ann met an author who invited her to join a "consciousness raising" group that met at the author's apartment. After the third meeting her hostess, Judy, suggested that she stay for a while after the meeting; and before many weeks passed, the two became fast friends. Ann was surprised to discover that Judy still counted her ex-husband, Dave, among her close friends. She was even more surprised, upon accepting Judy's invitation to spend the weekend with Judy's group at the shore, to discover the degree of intimacy in the group. She met Dave and his wife, another couple, and three other singles and was impressed with the sense of peerdom among them. It soon became apparent from their conversation that several of these individuals were sexually intimate and that this was considered acceptable behavior among this group of friends. There was no pressure on her to become sexually involved; but during subsequent conversations with Judy she indicated her interest in Judy's friends. One night, while sleeping over at Judy's apartment, she told Judy that she had been seeing Ken, one of the guys in the group, and that another one, Bud, had invited her to go road racing with him. Judy assured her that she need not worry about setting up a conflict.

Today, over a decade later, Ann is still a part of this intimate group. She and Bud have been married for four years now, and Judy is living with another member of the group who recently moved to New York. Some of the original members are now scattered about the country; but this has resulted in linking the group to other groups of intimate friends in other cities. Ann still has hopes of finding, someday, the right people to set up a complex living group, although she admits that it appears to be much easier said than done.

The kind of progression both Ann and Judy experienced, from one type of lifestyle to another, is the normal pattern for most Americans. The 1970 Census revealed that only about 37 per cent of the population lived in an "ideal" nuclear family of working father, housewife mother, and kids. Many, like Judy, went from a nuclear family to college dorm life to a childfree marriage and then became divorced singles who developed primary relationships outside marriage. Others, like Ann, have traveled from a dual-career family to college dorm life, have belonged to a complex living group and then moved to single status, and from there to cohabitation and then to marriage. There are hundreds of possible paths. The important thing to remember is that most Americans experience several of the wide range of non-nuclear family styles practiced in our country during their lifetimes. It has been suggested that if the current trend continues, we may be running out of families almost as fast as we are running out of oil. According to Conference Board projections, the number of Americans living alone is expected to climb to 16 million by 1980, assuming *no acceleration* of the existing trends (Etzioni, 1974). Today one out of three of the women in the 20–25 age group are still single. We will examine some of the reasons in more detail in the next chapter.

One way to simplify the process of making lifestyle choices is to gauge the degree of commitment that will be required by a potential relationship, whether individual or group, that you contemplate entering into. This process applies equally well to a friendship, an invitation to cohabit, a primary relationship or a complex living arrangement. On a scale of one to ten, ask yourself how close you feel to each person in the potential relationship along these intimacy vectors: social, sexual, emotional, intellectual, family, and work. Compare the results with the degree of commitment you believe will be expected of you in the potential relationship. How closely will you have to relate to each individual on each vector in order to satisfy *their* commitment expectations? Ask yourself if you are willing to make the investment of time and energy necessary to achieve that degree of commitment to the new relationship. Discuss the matter freely, thoroughly, and honestly with the others in the potential relationship. Remember, they will be reaching a decision about *your* becoming a part of the relationship too, so be sure you discuss *their* negatives about the potential relationship as well as your own. The positives always take care of themselves—it is the negatives you need to work out.

4

Power vs. Peerdom:
Is Honesty the Best Policy?

If the traditional nuclear family is as unstable as it appears to be, what steps can we take to make dyadic (two-person) relationships more stable? I first addressed this problem in a paper in 1960 entitled "Getting More Mileage From Your Marriage." At that time I was quite involved in organization and small group theory and was very impressed with Wiener's books, *Cybernetics. Control and Communication in the Animal and the Machine* (1948) and *The Human Use of Human Beings: Cybernetics and Society* (1950). The systems approach described by Wiener and others seemed especially well adapted to solving a basic problem in marriage—the difficulty in achieving any reasonable balance of power in the relationship. Many people were saying that a primary relationship *ought* to be democratic; but their prescriptions for how to achieve this utopian stage always boiled down to compromise. Compromise, of course, is a cop-out. Compromise means giving in, and guess who gives in, in marriage? In the 1950s, there was no question that it was the woman who compromised and the man who was "Master of his own house."

The paper I wrote in 1960 suggested both the use of cybernetic principles of control through feedback, synergistically building "critical mass" e.g., a good working relationship, through actively promoting individual growth and shared leadership, and the use of consensus (unanimous agreement) as the tool for achieving an equitable relationship. The resultant marriage type, which I later dubbed a "peer-bond" (1972a), was defined as one that "permits and promotes the growth of each partner in the relationship as well as the growth of the relationship itself." How does this system work?

A primary relationship can be thought of as a group of elements which are tied together through their communication with each other. This communication may be verbal or nonverbal and may also include the manner in which tasks are divided. Each individual in the relationship can be thought of as a similar group of elements tied together by internal communication. In other words, the individuals are autonomous parts of the partnership. In an organization, whether it is the functional parts of the human body or the partners in a primary relationship, the parts not only operate together in a communication network, they also exhibit another characteristic: They operate together to reach or maintain a set of goals. Their behavior may be interpreted as either purposeful, that is goal-directed, or purposeless, that is, not directed toward achieving these goals. Our concern at the moment is only with purposeful behavior in these terms.

Just as the individual has a set of both simple and complex goals, so does the partnership. For a peer primary relationship, such goals might include, for example, survival of the primary relationship, sharing household chores equitably, promoting the continuing growth of each partner, taking a vacation in Europe, and investing in antiques, among other things. Some of these goals are obviously much more complex than others.

In a traditional male-dominant relationship it is generally the woman who "compromises" or gives in, so that decisions are reached by compromising *her* position, thus allowing the male to "run away" with the relationship, since there is no governor on his actions. This either leads to her becoming completely submerged into her partner's will, and becoming a "handmaiden to God," or to a short marriage, because she becomes fed up and gets a divorce.

Classic perception studies suggest that if couples face a problem together rather than as protectors attempting to shield their mates from trouble, they will come closer together in their perceptions and consequently will be closer in their solutions. By substituting consensus for compromise, the couple can take the first step toward peer relating. Consensus means unanimous agreement. It requires a lot of discussion. This is why we say that at the heart of every peer relationship there is an ongoing dialogue through which the communication and debate that leads to consensus goes on. The requirements for this dialogue are that all input be considered legitimate, whether it be social, sexual, or career input, and that there be no secrets or holding back of input. If the partners observe these ground rules, then each gets constant feedback from the other with respect to his or her input as well as being fed new information from the other. "Dialogue may be regarded as *love in language,* since it hinges on mutuality, on loving the other as oneself, if it is to succeed. A dialogue-centered marriage offers a much greater chance of stability and a more satisfying framework for the nurture and growth of children" (Hobbs, in Otto, 1970).

This feedback is necessary for control. It is the way the partnership compares what it is doing, saying, and thinking with its goals. Using feedback, the partnership can detect any error or difference that might exist between the two partners, and through the interaction process, it can act to reduce that error. Thus feedback helps control both the behavior of each partner and the partnership itself. The feedback may be either negative or positive, of course, depending upon whether or not the behavior is found to be in accordance with the agreed upon goals. In this manner feedback is the governor that the couple uses *to maintain momentum under changing conditions,* which is the purpose of a governor, and the reason one would want to exercise control.

As problem-solving organisms, we humans have a highly developed ability to collect information, store it in memory, and then think about it for the purpose of formulating new courses of action. Imagine Joe about to step off the curb at an intersection. He sees that the walk signal has changed to "don't walk" but he knows how long it will take to cross the street if he hurries. Several cars are waiting to cross the intersection, and he notices that the one closest to the other side of the street is a taxi. He decides, upon reflection, that the cab driver may "jump the gun" on the traffic light. He steps back up on the curb and waits for the "walk" signal. Joe has been using his reflective goal-changing ability, or consciousness.

The individual consciousness, or the collective consciousness of the partnership, can select from all its input that information relevant to its goals. It can redirect attention, concentrate awareness on some factors and ignore others, initiate or cease courses of action, examine the status of its communicating process, search its collective memory, and pick up deviations between various actions and the goals which direct them. By taking such actions, the partnership can direct its own growth. Because it can recognize valuable information or combinations between new input and information already stored in memory, the partnership can innovate.

But what is to prevent this system from leading to the same kind of compromise behavior that one finds in a traditional marriage? We spoke in the first chapter of the "systems approach" study of family interaction which found that (1) it is impossible not to communicate, (2) the central issue in every communication is either reinforcing or attaining dominance or reinforcing/attaining equality, and (3) the primary relationship is a situation in which the couple must work out rules for living together as well as rules for making the rules. As you can see, we are now addressing the problem of how to insure that we attain and reinforce equality rather than dominance within the framework of this "change and conflict" model of primary relationships.

The key issue is personal freedom and autonomy. How do you arrive at a peer relationship if the male assumes the leadership role and his mate is left with the scut work? Leadership theory has undergone profound changes since World War II. People used to believe that leaders were born, not made, and that the "natural superiority" of the male made him the natural leader in the marriage. As a matter of interest, it was the need to find leaders to drop behind the lines to organize resistance forces in France that led the OSS to realize that they did not know how to choose leaders. They quickly discovered that all the known methods of predicting leadership were worthless. They then devised a method of discovering leaders in concrete situations. They might, for example, place fifteen men on one side of a deep ravine and tell them they had ten minutes to get across. It soon became apparent that in such instances, someone always seemed to come up with a solution to the problem; but it wasn't always the same person. They found, also, that a group would first turn to the person who had exercised "situational leadership" in the last test to see if he had a solution to the new problem. If not, the group quickly looked to others for solutions. Out of these early beginnings emerged a new concept—the concept of *leader behavior*. "Leader behavior is behavior that permits and promotes the growth of the group in a shared direction, thereby lending status to the leader in direct proportion to the degree and value of his active participation and demonstration of his capacity to cooperatively guide the group to successful achievement of its goals" (Ramey, 1960).

By recognizing that it is leader behavior, rather than the leadership of one individual, that is critical to maintaining a successful peer primary relationship and agreeing that each individual will exercise leader behavior according to his or her ability to solve the problem, it becomes possible for the couple to create a new way of relating. At the same time, each maintains autonomy because neither is constantly taking a subordinate or submissive role in the relationship. In this manner each partner continues to develop his or her own particular interests and abilities while contributing positively to the growth of the relationship.

This process of interaction or dialogue we call synergy, a process by which the whole becomes greater than the sum of its parts without changing the structure of those parts. It is the combination of feedback/control in this synergistic relationship that develops the "critical mass" that so obviously distinguishes a peer primary relationship from an ordinary primary relationship. If a couple reaches agreement on the basis of compromise, one partner changes structure, becoming submerged into the "couple" that is dominated by the other partner. If, however, the couple operates on the principles we have been discussing, they release energy by synergistically building both themselves and the relationship without submerging either partner in the "couple." Critical mass, in this context, is that vibrant state of energy release in a primary relationship that contributes to an ever-growing, expanding, jubilant life for the partners as well as for the partnership. Contrast this to Pineo's description (1961) of traditional marriage based on love and free choice: "Since the couple begins marriage at a high point of love and 'fit' between their personalities, they have nowhere to go but down." He called this the "disengagement" process. This happens because traditionally, as Skolnick (1973) notes, "marriage has never been defined as a partnership of two equal persons. In popular thought, in learned writing on the family, and most significantly, in terms of the law, marriage is a hierarchical institution defining the wife as the subordinate of the husband."

Nancy's concept of equality was "one for you and one for me," and she was determined to be Peter's equal in their new marriage. She soon discovered, however, that it was pretty tough to keep score of equivalent privileges. If Peter went to Philadelphia on business, had dinner in a fancy restaurant, and spent the evening taking a client to a play, was she entitled to an equivalent evening on the town? Who would go with her? Soon Peter and Nancy were doing everything together, because it was the only "fair" way to allocate resources. But this meant that she had to give up ballet lessons unless she was willing to let Peter continue practicing with his jazz group. Soon they were giving up a lot of things they had previously enjoyed, and restricting their growth to the few shared areas of interest. Before long, Nancy was blaming marriage for her own lack of personal freedom and for her feeling that she had stopped growing as an individual. She began to believe the notion that personal freedom and commitment are not compatible.

Where did Nancy and Peter go wrong? They started out with the desire for equality in their relationship; but they did not realize that equality promotes equilibrium, or a steady state, rather than growth. Equilibrium is a state of rest due to the action of forces that counteract each other. It is *not* a dynamic growth state. What Nancy and Peter should have considered was willingness to accept equity rather than equality, thus promoting morphogenesis. Morphogenesis is the dynamic process by which people change and modify their responses through dialogue, while maintaining their autonomy, thus keeping the relationship responsive to changes in the situation and in the environment. Each must give the other the freedom s/he seeks for himself; and moreover, each must take positive steps to help the other achieve his or her personal goals. One of the distinctive characteristics of a peer relationship is the degree to which the partners function as individuals, rather than on a "couple-front" basis. (See Speer, 1970 for a somewhat different tracking to a similar conclusion.)

Peer relating requires a great deal of trust, openness, and willingness to experiment. Most of all, it requires agreement on the ground rules by which the couple operates and on how those rules are set up and/or changed. *The time to start this process is before getting into the relationship.*

We begin to be socialized for marriage roles from early childhood. Boys are encouraged in aggressive behavior. Girls are encouraged to be passive and submissive. Boys are expected to be active and interested in play. Girls are expected to be emotional and loving and to cuddle. Maccoby and Jacklin's (1975) examination of all of the sex difference research, according to a review by Susan Edmiston (1975), reveals that "while there may be a few innate differences between boys and girls, there are not as many as we usually suppose; that while there may be some differential socialization on the part of parents they do not exert the overwhelming pressure we usually assume. It is instead the self-concepts of children that exert an influence we underestimate. There is nothing either male or female but thinking makes it so."

This self-concept explanation is based on Kohlberg's (1975) cognitive theory that the child develops the notion of what it means to be a boy or girl based on what it sees and hears. Even though male and female gender role ideas might not be heavily reinforced at home, and despite the existence of multiple role models, the external world certainly reinforces biased models of what it means to be male or female, particularly on television, in books, in school, and in the surrounding, male-dominant society. Current work with transsexuals has shown that even after three or four years a child can quickly and successfully shift from boy to girl role or vice versa when it has been discovered that their sex was wrongly determined at birth. This early gender role socialization quickly becomes overlaid with marriage role expectations. Little girls play house, while little boys play war. Even today, with our new awareness of the changes that are occurring in the psychology of women, society is still preparing them for the submissive marriage role and young people are having to fight an uphill battle to overcome the "imprinting" of years of marriage role socialization.

The surest way to deal with the power struggle is to get it out in the open before getting married. Once traditional marriage roles have been accepted it is exceedingly difficult, although not impossible, to throw them out and start over again from scratch. The dialogue on developing ground rules should start before the decision is made to cohabit if possible, and certainly before the decision to unite in a primary relationship is agreed upon.

Allen and Jean were both wary of remarriage. Jean's first marriage ended in divorce in less than a year, and she had stayed unmarried for five years before she met Allen. He had been widowed only six months before; and after four years of what he had considered to be a great marriage, he was convinced that any new relationship couldn't possibly measure up to the one he had experienced before. Nevertheless, the two found that they had much in common, much to share with each other, and tremendous respect for one another. Allen suspected that, in his case, it was "rebound," and he said so. Jean just as frankly indicated that she was probably overreacting in her feelings toward him because he wasn't put off by her aggressiveness and treated her like a person. They first began seriously talking about their feelings with respect to establishing primary relationships during a summer weekend of hiking in the hills by day and making love by night. The conversation sounded very negative, for each in turn talked about the things s/he would not put up with in a relationship, the habits and outside relationships s/he would not give up for anybody, the stiff resistance s/he would put up if anybody tried to change his or her personality or way of doing things. "I'm 29," Jean said, "and I know what I like and don't like, what I want and don't want, and I'm not about to give up anything for a man."

This conversation became a dialogue, for it did not stop at the end of their weekend outing. Each time they were together, and on the phone in between, they continued to talk about what they were unwilling to give up for the sake of a relationship. Gradually, out of this dialogue came a meeting of minds about the kind of ground rules a primary relationship would have to operate from in order to be viable for each of them. Over a period of three months they had hammered out enough common ground to be comfortable with cohabiting on a trial basis. Eight months later, on the advice of their tax accountant, they decided to get married; but by that time they had already established the kind of peer primary relationship that they felt was right for them, married or not.

In conversations with the author, Jean suggested that she and Allen had a big advantage over those who have never been married or in a primary relationship because each had already had such an experience before they met each other and hammered out their ground rules. But many who have not been previously married arrive at the same sort of verbal contract. Some even reduce them to writing. Those who have had cohabiting experiences in college *may* have some edge on this process; but as long as the couple approaches the subject in easy steps, as Jean and Allen did, it really doesn't matter what their previous experience has been. The real problems lie with those who begin a primary relationship first, and *then* try to work out the ground rules, or with those who think they had better not take a chance on rocking the boat until after they have the relationship "locked up," only to find out that what they really have done is to lock themselves in.

In any relationship, achieving and maintaining critical mass is important—remember, a relationship that is not growing is shrinking. There is no standing still in life. In a world of constant change you either go forward or you lose ground. This is the key to overcoming the built-in instability of the nuclear family that we discussed in Chapter One. You have to keep it moving, which means that the *partners* must each continue to grow. As long as they both grow, the interaction process that facilitates their growth will guarantee the continuing growth of their relationship.

If, however, they let the process grind to a halt, they will soon find themselves sliding back into the old traditional marriage roles. This may be very comforting to their parents, to their neighbors, and perhaps even to some of their friends—especially those who do not have peer primary relationships and who do not want to believe that such relationships can or will work for anyone. Much of their unhappiness will relate to the uncomfortable differences they perceive between the lifestyle of their own traditional relationship and the lifestyle of the partners in a peer relationship.

One of the most noticeable of these differences is the freedom of the peer partnership to break the couple-front. The couple-front is so axiomatic a part of being married, for traditional relationships, that traditional couples feel very threatened by couples who do not observe it. It is the symbol of their togetherness, and the symmetry is not accidental. Couples tend to relate to other couples and to be uncomfortable in the presence of singles because a single is a threat to the solidarity of the couple. This is why newly widowed or divorced persons are the subject of such an intensive campaign on the part of their friends to get them remarried, or at least recoupled, quickly. If this doesn't work, the friends tend to withdraw from their former friend, especially if she is female, "before my husband gets any ideas."

The freedom of individuals in a peer relationship to remain individuals in as many of their activities as they choose, even activities involving members of the opposite sex, causes consternation among friends and relatives alike. In America, we automatically assume that *any* interaction between two people of the opposite sex will end up in the bedroom. It is an asinine assumption, of course, a legacy of the extreme sexism of our advertising industry and our categorization of women as possessions. Nevertheless, this freedom from the obligatory couple-front is an important factor in helping to maintain personal freedom and autonomy in a peer relationship.

People in a peer relationship are also likely to have, as friends, singles of both sexes, not just other couples. And because they will probably choose new friends from among others with similar attitudes toward relating, they will have friends who are parts of couples. Some of these relationships may ultimately become quite intimate, perhaps even sexually intimate, but not necessarily so. The person-to-person relationship really is more important than, even if it includes, a genital-to-genital relationship. Furthermore, the friendship may exist for many years before sexual intimacy develops, if it ever does. As a result of their intense involvement with close friends, the peer couple is likely to seem unusually busy to their traditional friends.

Both are likely to be pursuing careers, and experiencing some problems with deciding whose career takes precedence in what situation. The wife's career is as likely as the husband's to be in academic, professional, managerial or creative work; and she is very likely to continue her education further than her traditionally married friends, with the full intention of practicing her chosen career for a lifetime. If the peer couple has arrived at the decision to establish a peer primary relationship through a reorganization of their marriage and a redefinition of the ground rules, the wife may begin educational preparation for a career at a point when other wives are still very involved with their pre-teen children. If their friends have teenage or college age children, the threat is even greater, for these traditional wives have nearly reached the point of feeling that they have lost their major function in life. My research indicates that very few peer wives settle for jobs as secretaries or other noncareer-oriented occupations, which makes the contrast stark between them and working wives in general. It can be upsetting for a man, let alone for his wife, to learn that his sister has been sent to Birmingham to set up a new plant for her company and expects to be there for six to ten months while her husband keeps the home fires burning in Chicago.

The peer couple is quite likely to avoid having children unless both partners feel that they really have some special talent for childrearing and that they have sufficient desire to rearrange their lives so that childrearing becomes more of an equal burden on *both* husband and wife. Assuming that the peer couple does have children, their childrearing attitudes will probably be noticeably different from those in traditional families. As soon as the child is out of the toddler stage, somewhere around age four, s/he is likely to be treated as a little person, given a great deal of freedom, but also expected to assume increasing responsibility not only for self but for the household. The child will be included in, rather than excluded from, family functioning, decision-making, and problems. This is especially likely to be the pattern if either parent has had complex living experience or if they are currently living in a complex arrangement. As Berger, Hackett, and Miller indicate in their report on child socialization in complex living situations: "The single most important belief governing the relation between children and adults is that the experiences had by children not be fateful or self-implicating for adults, that adults cannot be legitimately characterized in terms of what they do with or to their children—in rather clear contrast to middle class views in which the behavior of children reflects upon their parents who are in some sense responsible for it" (1972).

The peer couple, because of their career level, are quite likely to locate at some distance from their relatives and parents, and to move every few years as a consequence of their careers. The peer couple is very likely to experience a sort of "information gap" between themselves and their parents and some relatives, because they will be reticent about sharing the experiences of their lifestyle with these relatives, especially if they suspect that the information will not only be misunderstood, but cause pain. It is not unusual for children to grow away from their parents in terms of careers and world view; but such radically different conceptualizations of the primary relationship itself are a different phenomenon: Many peer couples find over time that there is almost complete withdrawal from family, especially parents, if the family members are unable to tolerate their attitudes about what is proper in a primary relationship. The surviving link is often the "ritual visit," maybe annually, perhaps timed to coincide with other visitors, and usually covering a time span no longer than the time it takes to catch up on all the news about what has happened to whom and to discuss other "safe" subjects. Parties or outings may be arranged to dilute conversation even further. Several research subjects have reported that for them, two and a half days is the limit on safe interaction; and their parents have sensed this limit as well as they, so that they get restless and find reasons to leave even if they have scheduled a longer stay.

If, on the other hand, the peer couple has teenage or grown children of their own, they report that it is much easier for them to communicate with their children than is the case for their friends in traditional marriages. Because they are more likely to be on the same wavelength with their children, they treat them as friends, and are puzzled about the so-called "generation gap" of which their neighbors complain. They are able to discuss freely the world as it actually exists, and especially the problems and attitudes and experiences they are having as well as those their children are having. This lack of barriers frees their children to be autonomous individuals and friends rather than dependents who must disguise their feelings and experiences and problems. At the same time, it frees the parents to share both their joyous world and their difficulties on an adult level with their children; also, the parents tend to be much more helpful to their children because they are willing to engage in a two-way dialogue rather than in a superior-subordinate inquisition and/or polite ignoring of reality, both of which are great detriments to the teenager.

The peer couple is likely to have a wider age range among their friends, especially if they are in their thirties or forties, and have practiced sexually open marriage for five or more years. In our sample of 380 individuals involved in intimate groups or networks, the age range was from 16 to 64, with an average age of 44 for the males and 40 for the females. Thirty-four were under 25, sixty-one between 25 and 34, 104 between 35 and 44, 119 between 45 and 54, and 62 over 54. This skew toward older participants was built into the study. We were already aware of a number of intimate groups and networks among people in their twenties and so we looked for much older people in similar networks. Nevertheless, when we then charted the groups and networks in which we found these individuals, twenty-five per cent of the members turned out to be under 35. Individuals in peer marriages appear much more likely to be sexually open in later years than most people.

The distribution of housekeeping roles is likely to be noticeably different in a peer marriage. Husbands may do some or much or even all of the cooking, shopping and cleaning. In many peer households the general rule is that whoever gets home first does what needs to be done to get dinner started. The distribution of other chores often proceeds along the lines of "least distaste for the task."

Peer couples tend to see themselves as the wave of the future and some of them may openly promote their way of life. They are likely to be leaders in the community, to see themselves as adaptable to change, as growth oriented, as able to cope with life as it comes, and as risk takers. They seem self-assured, self-reliant, and satisfied with their lifestyle; and on the whole, they seem to be creative individuals. They view life and love as an open-ended affair, in which the giving of one's self and one's love adds to the store of life and love to give. This is in distinct contrast to those who view love as a zero-sum game—a finite "pie" that can only be divided and sub-divided, so that to give to one takes from another. The partners in a peer primary relationship see each other as intimate friends and lovers who maintain their relationship because they want to, not because they are obliged to. This is perhaps the most telling difference from those in traditional marriages who feel trapped because they suspect that they would be unable to cope with the "outside world" alone.

Of course, all these differences between peer and traditional relating apply equally to those in more complex living arrangements, which can be just as traditional as any marriage or just as liberating as the kind of peer relationship we have talked about in this chapter.

5

Married vs. Single: Is This the Right Question to Ask Today?

Russ got his bright idea at 4:30 Wednesday afternoon and called Cathy to suggest getting some of the gang together for an old fashioned weenie and marshmallow roast. She agreed to call Bill and Harvey and Silvia, and he called Ellen and Dan and Jerry and Arnie. That evening three cars and a Jeepster headed for the Forest Preserve. The spontaneous outing was a smashing success, and it was almost three in the morning when they headed for home.

Who are these people? Russ is a 28-year-old lawyer, and his wife Cathy, 27, is a research chemist. Bill, 32, is a hospital administrator who lives in a threesome with 52-year-old Ross, a doctor, and 42-year-old Rose, a nursing administrator. Harvey, at 25 the youngest member of the group, is a doctoral candidate in embryology, and he brought Susan, a 30-year-old TV news editor with whom he is living at the moment. Ellen, although 38, is a college sophomore, now that her children are out of the nest. She had to come alone because her husband, Hank, age 40, had to attend a planning board meeting. Russ barely caught Dan, a 56-year-old professor, before he left the campus with a briefcase full of papers to grade. Dan and his wife Cindy, who at 50 heads her own architecture firm, had planned to go out and celebrate his new grant award the next evening, but they decided to switch things around, celebrating tonight with marshmallows and grading papers the next night. Forty-five-year-old Jerry, program director at a radio station, picked up Ann, 33, and her husband Arnie, 48, at their antique shop, which rounded out the group except for Silvia, 55, and John, 61, who recently took early retirement from his Civil Service job.

What did all of these people have in common? The ability to change their plans at the ring of a telephone at 4:30 on a Wednesday afternoon and set out on a lark that kept them all up until four o'clock in the morning. Ten of the sixteen are married and three are living in what the group considers to be a long-term relationship. Silvia and John have teenage grandchildren; Arnie has a daughter in college by his first wife; and Ellen and Hank, the most recent additions to the group, wish that they had been as fortunate as Cathy and Russ in avoiding children. They are only now enjoying the postchildrearing freedom they have looked forward to for so many years. Russ and Cathy haven't actively decided against kids; but they have no immediate plans for any either, especially with Cathy about to be promoted to Department Head. The striking thing about the lifestyles of these people—unmarried singles, young marrieds without children, postchildrearing parents, a deliberately child-free couple, and retirees—is their similarity.

Betty and Tod are in the thick of childrearing. This morning she is at her wits' end. The baby's prescription ran out and the druggist can't deliver today because his delivery person is ill. The baby must have the medicine every two hours, so Betty has a choice. Find a sitter or go herself. After thirty frantic and fruitless minutes on the phone, trying to find someone to stay with her children, Betty puts Sammy's sweater, boots, parka, cap, and gloves on and then dresses the baby to go out, sick or not, to the drugstore—a ten minute drive. While trying to dress the baby she wonders to herself why she listened to the "expert advice" that led to spacing the kids two years apart.

Before leaving the house, Betty stops the laundry cycle and

supper preparation because she knows she cannot count on being gone only 20 minutes. Once out the door, she realizes that the delivery man from Sears will probably show up and leave unless she alerts him to leave her vacuum sweeper outside the door. It has been in the repair shop for two weeks already and if she misses him she will have to wait another week for a delivery to her area. She writes a note, finally locates some plastic tape to stick it on the door, puts it up, and then discovers that Sammy has lost one of his gloves. Five minutes later, as she is about to drive away, she hears the phone ringing. She rushes back into the house but it stops ringing. When she finally gets to the drugstore, the prescription isn't ready.

Betty can remember when she and Tod had the kind of happy-go-lucky lifestyle enjoyed by their former neighbors, Cathy and Russ. Sammy's arrival changed all that. Somehow there is never enough time. They gave up their lovely apartment on the near North Side for a house in the suburbs because it would be better for raising children. The savings account practically disappeared overnight as they faced the necessity of buying two cars, since the nearest store was in a shopping center two miles away and there is no public transportation to take Tod into the city to work. They had to buy additional furniture so the house wouldn't look so bare; and then there was the 34 per cent increase in their taxes three months after they moved in—and that was only the beginning. Suddenly all the things the Super had taken care of became her responsibility, and she seemed to be on the phone constantly, calling Tod long-distance at his office in the city, to find out how to handle a new emergency.

She was so busy with the house and with Sammy that at first she didn't notice that they didn't see their old friends much anymore. But she did notice that it became more and more difficult to keep up with her career. She had been so sure that, as a graphic artist, she could continue to freelance and maintain some earnings and contact with her career; but she found that she just couldn't concentrate on work in the face of motherhood and household demands. She gave up the work rather than face the embarrassment of repeated failures to make deadlines. By this time Sammy was a little over a year old and getting into everything, and she was pregnant again. They had just gotten to the stage where she and Tod could at least get away now and then and trust Sammy with a sitter.

But if one child was difficult, two were almost impossible. Tod wanted to be helpful, but there was little he could do. After fighting rush-hour traffic for 90 minutes just to get home, he was worn out, too, and he had to leave at seven A.M. to get to work. Nothing happened spontaneously anymore except emergencies. Housecleaning, that had once been a two hours now-and-then task that they did together, became an unending task, with two little ones to clean up after constantly. Meals were no longer easy to fix at odd hours, and were no longer punctuated by trips to the pizza parlor or a candlelight affair at the little French restaurant. Cooking was almost constant, sometimes for two, three, four or more, and each with a different menu. The washer and dryer were in use every day and the only adults Betty saw were on TV.

Living constantly in a child's world was more than debilitating. She felt that it was addling her brain. There was absolutely no respite. They did all shopping in one trip a week, to economize, which further limited adult company for Betty. When she began to feel desperate—as if that wasn't enough—Tod was promised a promotion if he completed his CPA exams, which added tremendously to the tension in the house. He couldn't study until after the kids went to sleep; and even though she at first tried to feed them before he got home and then eat with him, that didn't work out because the children constantly interrupted during their parents' meal, so she finally began eating with them and then taking them in and putting them to bed while Tod ate alone. This meant seeing him for a few minutes while he hurried through his breakfast and for a few more minutes before he went to sleep. The weekends were worse. The only way he could study then was to go to the library on Saturday and stay until closing.

We have all been socialized to divide people into two groups—married and single. In today's world, we need to re-examine that division, for now it makes more sense to think in terms of adult-centered living and child-centered living. Clearly Betty and Tod live in a child-centered universe. They *must* evaluate everything they do in terms of the effect on the children. If they want to go somewhere, they must either take the children or find a babysitter, which may take an hour or more and may prove fruitless altogether. They have stopped seeing their old crowd and restrict themselves to visiting their parents or other people with children of approximately the same age—not because their old friends have abandoned them, but because they do not want to impose their children, and their children's demands, on people whose homes are not set up to handle children. Betty is secretly terrified that Tod's promotion will involve a move out of town, away from their parents. Both sets of grandparents are now within a two hour drive, and even at that distance it is a blessed relief to be able to leave the children with them once in a while. In spite of this, most of the things Betty and Tod once enjoyed together have become such an effort that they just don't bother anymore.

We have always automatically divided society into the married and unmarried in the past because we assumed that only misfits and oddballs remained single as adults. In our society a single person was without status because s/he was considered to be not a whole person. Our laws and customs were, and still are, for the most part, geared to the assumption that people live in male/female pairs. Thus we discriminate against those who do not (although the 1970 Census found 37 million single adults— 25 per cent of the adult population). One of the reasons was, of course, that people are supposed to live in nuclear families. Until very recently, no matter how long a couple had been married, they were not considered a family unless the wife was "fulfilled" by having children.

Many changes have occurred and are occurring to change the way it was. Today one out of every ten white children under sixteen lives in a single parent family and three of every ten black families are headed by women in single parent households. In 1965 in Oregon a 38-year-old bachelor musician named Tony Piazzam became the first male in the United States to adopt a child legally. By 1974, it was possible not only for both single males and females to adopt, but also for acknowledged homosexuals to adopt.

It has become possible not only to raise children outside the married state, but also to bear them without the intense stigma of past years. Not only prominent individuals in the entertainment world but ordinary people as well are having children out of wedlock deliberately. The number of unwed mothers had increased by 80 per cent between 1965 and 1972 alone (U.S. Census Bureau), although the nationwide availability of abortion has since reversed this trend.

Two biological developments, positive contraception (the pill and the intrauterine device) and permanent contraception (vasectomy and laparoscopy or tubal ligation) have completely changed the scenario with respect to marriage and having a family. A legal development, legalized abortion on demand, has added to the change. Sexuality is clearly no longer a by-product of conception. Making love because you want to and not in order to have children can be undertaken safely and may be under the complete control of the woman. Already the first fruits of this new found freedom from the fear of conception are showing up in the statistics at the National Population Center in the form of more reported intercourse by women in all age groups. Already the majority of those practicing contraception are using either the pill, the IUD, or sterilization; and for those married couples where the wife is past her 29th year, the preferred single method, used by one out of four couples in 1970, was sterilization.

The impact of these changes in the ability to control conception on our society is indicated by the previously mentioned Institute of Life Insurance national survey carried out in 1973, which found that three out of four respondents agreed that it was perfectly all right for married couples to choose not to have children. Furthermore, the childbearing years have been reduced to the ten years between age 20 and 30. As a result of these changes it becomes feasible, in the decade of the 1970s, for many people to do what a few had long advocated and some had actually done: separate childbearing/rearing from relating sexually without the intent to produce children.

In 1890 Mona Caird strongly advocated trial marriage as a nonprocreative activity and was roundly condemned for her views. In the 1920s Judge Ben Lindsey read her articles and began speaking and writing in favor of companionate marriage. These two terms were approximately synonyms since they both involved marriage for less than a lifetime which specifically avoided conception. The judge lost his judgeship in the national uproar over his advocacy of such a "sinful" union. Nevertheless, in the 1920s many people quietly listened to the judge's advice, found it good, and acted upon it. Within a couple of decades it was tacitly understood that an "engaged" couple were probably sexually involved before marriage, and an increasing number of people cohabited for some time before marriage. Of course, there was the chance that cohabitation would not lead to marriage, but this aspect of cohabitation was not usually discussed. Thus, in the Cornell study in 1974, as we have previously indicated, two-thirds of the parents of college students in the study were aware of cohabitors among members of their own generation.

Until the advent of the pill, however, the risk of getting pregnant was so great that many cohabitors wound up married in order to avoid bastardy for their offspring. Once it *was* possible to control conception, there was no longer any biological reason not to cohabit; and the practice quickly became so widespread that in 1971 the New Hampshire State Legislature actually voted on a bill stipulating that "unattached" couples living together for thirty days "shall be deemed to be married" as far as "all the obligations of support" are concerned (Francoeur, 1972).

In 1969 Jetse Sprey suggested a conceptual framework for research which saw sexuality as an emerging autonomous institution which was not tied to reproduction and childrearing. The following year a Methodist theologian predicted that "in the near future, United States marriage will be as in all societies, the institution whereby men and women are joined for the purpose of founding and maintaining a family. This special kind of dependence, however, will be limited to reproduction of offspring by the couple. Sexual relationships will not be limited to the marriage bond in any special way whatever, except of course that pregnancy control will always be maintained in or out of the marriage except when children are planned as a result" (Hobbs in Otto, 1970).

Perhaps the widest circulation for a proposal of this nature resulted from Margaret Mead's *Redbook* article in 1966 in which she proposed two-step marriages. In the initial step, marriage would be public, but would involve an ethical rather than an economic responsibility, and positive contraception would be required. Her second step was called "parental marriage" and was to be entered into for the specific purpose of having children. Only those who had been successful in a first-step marriage would be allowed to undertake a parental marriage and they would be required to demonstrate economic ability to support a family. Mead specifically identified first-step, or "individual" marriage with Judge Lindsey's "companionate" marriage and recognized that it would be a short term relationship for most people. In Sweden the government has already changed the law to recognize marriage as only one of the many possible ways people may cohabit. Swedish children are legitimated under other legal provisions.

In 1970, Cuber also suggested that some changes be made in our system of marriage and legitimation of children. He called for legal recognition of all of the marriage alternatives actually being practiced, arguing that an open system would reduce the motivation for deceptive practices and that the individual's self-concept would improve if actual behavior was not proscribed.

Leo Davids (1974) sees a future in which only twenty-five or thirty per cent of the population will feel so serious a need to have children that they will go through the extensive training and evaluation that will then be required to be licensed as parents, much as we now subject potential adoptive parents to rigorous investigation and evaluation. He would agree with

Keller (1971) that "maternity, far from being a duty, not even a right, will then become a rare privilege to be granted to a select and qualified few."

By 1973, 27 per cent of Americans already approved cohabitation out of wedlock, and the idea of reserving wedlock for raising a family seemed to be spreading. Clearly the individual has more choices available than ever before for experimenting with a number of relationship possibilities—and there is less likelihood of getting "trapped" into parenthood than ever before.

My continuing study of intimate groups and networks among both upper-middle class adults and younger groups of college students and their noncollegiate peers as well as individuals now in their late twenties and thirties, some of whom were college students and some not, indicates that we may already be shifting rapidly toward the pattern of diverse interaction between people of all ages who may or may not be married but who are not currently child-centered. There may be a short detour into a child-centered state for some of these people, who rejoin the adult-centered world much sooner than was the case in the past, when the child-centered era lasted for about 18 to 20 years per child. Depending on socio-economic level, parents in these intimate groups and networks are now restricting their child-centered years to perhaps half as many as before. Many are conscious of the drastic difference between having one child, "which it is possible to work around," and having more than one, "which forces the parents to give up any idea of remaining adult-centered until the youngest child is at least ten." I have found some evidence of both exclusion of child-centered individuals from adult-centered intimate groups and networks and of self-exclusion or banding together of child-centered couples and singles into their own intimate groups, which may form links with adult-centered networks later on during the postchild-centered years. In one adult-centered network, parents have deliberately restricted themselves to a single child in order not to sacrifice relationships built up over many years. Even with only one child, however, they experience considerable loss of mobility and must make great efforts to do justice to the child without allowing themselves to lose their essentially adult-centered perspective.

Living in a complex group greatly simplifies the effort, of course. One group of eight adults, involving three married couples and two singles, one of each sex, all employed, has a full-time housekeeper and more than enough adults to share care for the three children. The adults range in age from 28 to 53 and the children from six to ten. For a group of this size, child care simply isn't a problem. It is unlikely that all eight adults would ever want to go out at the same time without the children, and if they did, the housekeeper could sit for them. This group is typical of the middle class nondropout complex living group in that it came into being as a means of optimizing ability to compete within the system.

Child-centered intimate groups frequently use the group as a family extension, exchanging children, relieving each other of the burden now and then, and providing kinship-type family support for each other. This is especially important to female single parent family heads. In child-centered intimate groups, as in adult-centered ones like the one described at the beginning of this chapter, however, the glue that binds people together, despite differences in age, sex, race, or sexual proclivity, is the fundamental philosophy expressed by a Unitarian minister, Ronald Mazur (1973): "What is universal or normal in human sexual behavior is for two persons to need each other for mutual sensual enjoyment. Nothing in human nature requires that two persons engaged in such pleasure be of different sexes. Human beings are human beings, and however they may please, comfort, support, inspire, or love each other is of human value."

When all is said and done, being child-centered is in one's head. We have seen in this chapter that it is possible to have children and still remain essentially adult-centered. We have also seen that it is not absolutely essential that one be married to act on one's desire to bear and raise children, although it is certainly more difficult to go it alone. If, therefore, we are right about the increasing blurring of the distinction between "married" and "single" then it is more than likely that the pressure will continue to mount toward reserving some sort of special distinction for parenting, whether married or unmarried, with a concurrent reduction in the distinction between married and unmarried individuals who are not involved currently in the parenting role.

Distinguishing Transitional from Traditional Relationships

In 1970, 36 per cent of the adult population was either single (25 per cent), widowed, separated or divorced (11 per cent). The ratio of unmarried to married adults is increasing rapidly; more of these individuals are considering their options in the light of the questions raised in Part I about where marriage is coming from, about the technological, biological, and sexual revolutions, and about the impact of this different world view on the individual. Additionally, many married people are also taking a new look at their situation vis-à-vis these changes.

In Part II we will consider some of the key factors that these individuals must process to their own satisfaction in arriving at decisions about what they want from relationships and what kind of relationships they want. As Bob Francoeur said (1972): "I am convinced that today's youth, conditioned to change, are really the first generation capable of viewing marriage as a process of personal and mutual growth within the total context of one's lifelong development as a person." The available evidence suggests that he has shortchanged the prior generations, for we find that at least among the upper-middle class, a remarkable capability for viewing all sorts of interpersonal relationships in this manner already exists.

6

Personal Growth and Autonomy: Can the Individual Flourish in Harness?

The idea that marriage or any other type of primary relationship should permit, much less promote, personal growth is a rather new one. As recently as the post-World War II era, "togetherness" was the word of the day; and togetherness left little room for independence, let alone personal growth. It was the relationship that was important, and individual growth was seen as a potential threat to togetherness. During those same years a similar theme was stressed in the world of work. It was the day of the "organization man"—one who was expected to conform to the needs of the organization. Perhaps these pressures were holdovers from a nation at war, when feeling ran high that "pulling together" was necessary for national survival. Much of this stress on togetherness at home and at work died down within the decade of the fifties, however, although it hasn't entirely disappeared. Today the more common American theme of individualism appears to be stronger than ever.

Personal growth is at the very heart of being human. The need to solve ever-higher levels of problems is the key factor that distinguishes us from the lower animals. Whether or not that is the case, there can be no doubt that humans are happiest when they are solving more and more complex problems. Many aphorisms, such as "the old rocking-chair will get you," express the idea that we stop growing when we stop this process. Each of us knows people who have been content to let habit take over most day-to-day decisions quite early in life, while others are still breaking new ground in their eighties. When we reach a level in a given area that is sufficiently satisfying, we let habit take over, restricting further growth for as long as we are pleased with the status quo in that area. This allows us to focus our energy on growth in other areas.

Personal growth has become an issue in marriage only recently. In the past, personal growth was a male prerogative. With a few notable exceptions, females were excluded from most careers, from politics, and from community affairs. Male freedom to grow in the social and sexual areas was guaranteed by the double standard, which is still built into most of our social institutions and is almost universally sanctioned. A woman is expected to subordinate her own individual needs to facilitate her husband's growth. Assuming women have equal rights to growth in all aspects of living, even including the social and sexual areas, it becomes apparent that such growth is almost impossible in a traditional monogamous marriage.

Traditional marriage provides the humorist with much material emphasizing how women are "kept in their places," that is, not allowed to grow. There is the well-known "Washington syndrome": many Congressmen divorce their wives after going to Washington "because their wives didn't keep up"—they didn't grow as fast or as far as their husbands. This is hardly surprising if women spend much of their time with small children and are forced to communicate with the adult world through their husbands. Adult interaction spurs growth.

In marriage or in any primary relationship, personal growth should be possible for as long as each partner desires and in whatever direction seems desirable. This is the self-actualizing ingredient that transforms pair-bonds into peer-bonds. However, peer relationships are a lot easier to discuss than to achieve. The temptation to backslide into traditional marriage husband–wife roles is as great for females as for males, particularly in the light of outside pressures to conform to societal stereotypes. Friends and family may be less than helpful. Building and maintaining a peer relationship is an unending task; but it is supremely rewarding for those who enjoy the challenge of personal growth, for themselves and their partners.

> When Martha and Pete talked about "life after graduate school" with Sue and Harry from across the hall, it was always assumed that each would be offered jobs in the same area. As matters turned out, Sue and Martha both got offers as clinical psychologists in Kansas City, while Pete was offered a terrific job in Minneapolis and Harry a post in the City Planning Office in St. Louis. Sue immediately cancelled her acceptance of the Kansas City job to go with Harry to St. Louis. She was amazed to learn that Martha was not planning to give up her position, too, in order to be with Pete. "After all, you two are *married*," Sue said, as though that were the key issue. "I'm not even married to Harry, but I think I owe him at least that much!"

Sue's acceptance of the traditional "wither thou goest, I go" belied the peer relationship she and Harry had originally set out to achieve, not because she went with him to St. Louis, but because she did so without really making a decision about the matter. Dual-career couples who believe in maintaining a peer relationship often face difficult decisions of this type, and it is not out of the question for some to set up two different domiciles for a time, despite the extra living, travel, and communication costs.

We are not talking about an isolated problem. Forty-four per cent of all females are now employed outside the home and three out of five working women are married. Three out of ten working women are strongly committed to careers. Fifty per cent of the housewives say they plan to work (Dept. of Labor). This is one facet of a larger area of concern, however—the need for personal autonomy.†The need to achieve autonomy is especially important to women, for men already have it. By autonomy we do not mean independence only. Independence is often assumed to mean "freedom from," in this case suggesting that somehow the primary relationship is the important thing, as though it has a life of its own and that the people involved live in a kind of symbiosis and would be unable to survive outside the relationship.

By autonomy we mean a self-contained, self-directed ability to function without leaning on anyone else. As the O'Neills' put it in *Open Marriage*, an open (or peer) marriage cannot exist unless both partners are secure in their personal identities. Men are already independent, as are many women, when they consider entering into a primary relationship; but whereas the man acquires a cook, housekeeper, and wife for the price of a little more responsibility, the woman sacrifices her self-identity—first upon giving up her name, and later upon giving up her ideas, values, and beliefs in favor of her husband's (de Beauvoir, 1953). Furthermore, she does so knowing that the odds are only one in two that the relationship will survive. Even in homosexual relationships we generally see this automatic adoption of husband-wife roles. Very infrequently do we think of people who are getting married as embracing co-equal or peer roles.

Women who are already in the subordinate role of wife in a traditional marriage face a very difficult task when they attempt to change the status quo. They run the grave risk of simply ending the relationship in divorce rather than changing the rules in the middle of the game. This is even more the case if they have already made the further step of embracing the much more dependent role of mother. Again, the man remains independent and autonomous even though he becomes a father, for he simply takes on more financial responsibility; while the woman takes on all the problems of childbearing/rearing, is further "chained to the home," and is removed from adult companionship and interaction. She thus becomes even more dependent on the man both financially and psychologically. It is, therefore, not surprising to find that few mothers of young children feel themselves to be in a position to press for greater autonomy in the primary relationship.

A young woman remarked to me recently that as a teenager she had a feeling that people in their twenties really had it all together. They seemed so much more mature. Now a few years past twenty, she has decided that most people don't mature at all—"they just mellow and slow down." Maturity is the mark of personal growth toward autonomy and self-actualization. One may choose to stay single and thus avoid the wife and hand-maiden trip. Forty-nine million Americans are single, widowed, or divorced today. In ten years the number of single men and women under thirty-five has doubled. Furthermore, singleness does not preclude parenthood. Far from it. One of every six minors in the country lives in a single parent household. But for those who wish to share the joys and sorrows of growth, and indeed, for those who are interested in establishing a relationship that will guarantee growth, a peer primary relationship is the most viable two-person relationship on the horizon. Such a relationship centers on an ongoing dialogue between the partners that accepts anything and everything as legitimate input. A relationship without secrets. A relationship that presumes no deceptive communication. Why is ongoing dialogue important?

While studying nonverbal communication, Birdwhistell (1967) found that the average married couple engages in 27½ minutes of conversation per *week!* People in traditional marriages progressively cut down on verbal input and depend more on nonverbal communication. The male does not appreciably change his habits or activities outside the house, but he carefully censors what he says about them at home. His wife may be aware that he is doing so, but she doesn't verbalize her knowledge. Over time, more verbal input is withheld and there is a greater reluctance to ask questions or enter into discussions that might lead to embarrassing situations. As they come to know each other better, safe areas are "talked out"; and after they establish living routines, there is little to talk about in these areas as well. Eventually they have little to say to each other, much less anything to discuss.

The initial error in this scenario is the decision to limit areas considered legitimate for discussion and to indulge in deceptive communication, usually in the mistaken assumption that it is "kinder" to do so.

Jane didn't tell Bob about her brief but torrid affair with Jack in her junior year, fearing he might not marry a nonvirgin. For two years she has lived with the constant fear that a chance remark by someone in their crowd regarding her former relationship with Jack might light a fuse under her marriage.

It takes a lot of guts to "tell it like it is" right from the beginning, but nothing can contribute more to knowing where you stand than being honest all the way. If a new and tentative relationship cannot stand the truth it will not survive the same truth later on.

Deceptive communication becomes a more serious problem after marriage. Soon newlyweds begin lying to accommodate to power conflicts in early marriage (Goodrich, Ryder, and Raush, 1968).

The problem begins with traditional dating and courtship ground rules. One "puts one's best foot forward" both in presentation of self and in response to the person being courted. A web of half-truths and deceptive communication builds up that progressively isolates people behind facades that carry over into marriage, assuming the couple gets married. Numerous reports on trial marriage and cohabitation on the college campus indicate that the desire to cut through the pretense and illusion of the courtship routine is a significant factor in the growing popularity of cohabitation (Berger, 1971; Macklin, 1974).

A relationship that is built on a no-secrets agreement must also consider all input legitimate; this ensures meaningful dialogue, which may be painful as well as pleasurable, the exact opposite of the traditional model. Nevertheless, willingness to consider all kinds of input, sexual as well as social and career, guarantees personal growth through the ensuing interaction. Such a relationship, as we have previously indicated, permits and promotes the growth of each individual and of the relationship itself. As each partner brings fresh input to their dialogue, new insights emerge and each partner must constantly re-evaluate his or her position vis-à-vis the new understanding. Each must learn to accept differences as well as agreements. Each must trust the other enough to reveal negative as well as positive feelings:

weaknesses, fantasies, lapses, failures, and goofs. Working through the negatives will resolve the problems.

Trust is a two-way street. We trust. We want to be trusted. But you are not likely to find two-way trust unless you find peers in the relationship. The blind trust of the handmaiden to God is childlike and immature, yet even a handmaiden cannot afford complete honesty. We say: "Don't tell him more than he needs to know." If you are dependent on a master you have to watch your step. Nor is the dominant male likely to reveal all to his handmaiden. He avoids "burdening" her with things "she wouldn't be interested in anyway." If he trusted her with potentially damaging information and the relationship turned sour, she might "hang" him with it. Only equals are likely to trust each other enough to tell each other the truth. Being independent partners implies more than simply being able to trust, however.

The very words "peer relationship" imply that each partner is autonomous: in a position to end the relationship if at any time it no longer seems satisfying. As we have previously indicated, three factors in today's world make it possible for the female to achieve such autonomy: positive contraception, economic self-sufficiency, and the psychological emancipation that has been so long in coming. Nevertheless, female autonomy in a relationship is difficult to achieve and maintain. Much that has been learned in the past must be unlearned before new approaches can be developed. Just learning to initiate—to speak up—is difficult. Many women have been trained to be agreeable, to speak only when spoken to, and to voice opinions only about trivial matters. It becomes difficult to know if there is a meeting of minds when one party suspects that the other may be agreeing only to be agreeable.

In the tenth year of their marriage, Dick came home from a business trip feeling so guilty about having gone to bed with an associate that he initiated a discussion with Marty, his wife, which led to their agreement that each was free to engage in outside sexual activity. Dick wasn't sure if Marty really agreed or if she simply wished him to know indirectly that she was not threatened by what he had done. Two small children and homemaking activities took up most of Marty's time and she rarely saw other adults except together with Dick. When the children were old enough to visit Grandma for a summer week, Marty informed Dick that she planned to spend a couple of days at the shore with a male friend of the family. Dick suddenly had a lot of re-evaluating to do.

Dick's situation illustrates the other side of the coin. As one partner becomes more autonomous, reality changes for the other as well, and both must deal with the change. Accepting an idea intellectually is very different from experiencing it at gut level. This accommodation to a different reality is in most instances a male problem, because it is usually the female who is struggling to become more autonomous. As suggested in the case of Dick and Marty, it is usually the male who initiates discussion leading to transmarital intimacy, whereas it is often the woman who takes the first active step to fulfill the agreement, often to the dismay of her spouse. However, one should not forget that the male often initiated the discussion because of his guilt feelings about secret extramarital activity.

As we have indicated before, peer marriage is not necessarily sexually open marriage, especially during the formative stages of the relationship. It takes time for two people to establish a relationship that each feels is equitable and comfortable. Many couples who have lived in a traditional marriage that ended in divorce approach the possibility of establishing a peer relationship with their eyes open to many of the pitfalls and problems they will have to overcome. Others decide to hack out new growing space in an existing traditional marriage and gradually convert it into a peer marriage. This process may take several months or several years. Most couples concentrate attention on each other during this critical period, building the peerdom they seek in a primary relationship. A few continue to be sexually open right from the beginning, in spite of the threat this poses to the new peer primary relationship.

The woman bears the brunt of re-evaluating roles in the

development of autonomy. Attention often focuses first on housework. (The majority of working wives continue to do 80 per cent of the household chores!) A simple way to redistribute household tasks is as follows: List each task on a separate 3 X 5 card or slip of paper. Each partner, in turn, takes these cards and ranks them. To do this, select the most desirable task. Then select the least desirable. Put these two cards aside and repeat the process with the remaining cards. When all the cards have been put in rank order from most to least desirable, write down the list on a sheet of paper. Now the other partner repeats this exercise. Upon comparing the lists, it will be seen that each partner prefers certain tasks that the other dislikes. This method reduces the number of tasks that must be handled in some equitable way because neither partner likes them; perhaps these can be handled either by rotation, by farming out to a professional cleaning service, or in some other mutually agreeable fashion.

What matters is not who does what, but how each feels about it. Where the woman indicates that she is most comfortable keeping the homemaker roles for herself, it is necessary to examine the basis for this decision to insure that it is not based on guilt, on a sense of inadequacy outside the house, or on outside pressure to conform to the female role. If she truly prefers to keep house, conclusions about the nature of her primary relationship are impossible until one has examined other aspects of that relationship.

Another female role with significant bearing on achieving autonomy in the primary relationship (with a male) is childbearing/rearing, as in the case of Betty and Tod, discussed earlier. This has become such an issue with young women in the past few years that, as previously mentioned, $33\frac{1}{3}$ per cent are now remaining single in the 20–25 age group. In one study (1965) it was found that one out of ten college students wanted no children; but by 1970 one out of four said they did not want children (*U.S. News & World Report*; Francoeur). Today, in an overpopulated world in which positive contraception is possible, we can establish primary relationships for the benefit of the adult partners in that relationship. It is no longer considered a calamity if a woman does not have children or a man does not perpetuate his line. We can be responsive to the living—to the now—rather than spend a major portion of our lives in incubation for the future. The current mobility of our society is one of the often overlooked precursors of this new attitude. Removed from the external pressures of family, friends and neighbors, it is much easier to resist the subtle and not so subtle pressures toward motherhood. Living in a strange community also exerts pressure toward working outside the home, not only because there are additional costs associated with living in a new place, but also because it is a crushing bore to stay home alone. As long as there are no children in the home, the couple has an adult orientation, and the resulting adult activities are very different from those of the child-centered person.

Only in the past decade has there been any legitimacy attached to not having children. In the past, it was unthinkable. People who disliked kids or didn't feel that they would make good parents had to pretend physical disability in order to explain their childless marriages. In Colonial times, marriage was conditional on pregnancy, for having children was the reason for getting married. Only a mother was a "whole" woman; and if one did not embrace motherhood wholeheartedly one suffered massive guilt feelings.

Currently, the number of American married couples who are choosing not to have a child at all has tripled in six years (*Newsweek*, 1973). Both the age of the couple and the number of their children at time of sterilization are continuing to decrease. If the current trend continues to grow, vasectomy and tubal ligation or laparoscopy will soon become the preferred means of contraception for everybody, because it is permanent. Of course not everyone who practices sterilization as a means of contraception is childless. Quite to the contrary. But the practice is growing fast among those who want to insure that there will be no accidents. "Better sterilization than abortion," say many young women who are concerned about the side effects of the pill and the IUD. Several groups have formed to provide forums for discussing the pros and cons of voluntary childlessness and providing mutual support when outside pressures mount in favor of having children. The most widely known group is the National Organization for Nonparents, or NON.

Most of the individuals who read these words already have children or plan to have at least one. For the women, achieving autonomy will mean developing ways of surviving as a whole person while at the same time coping with the difficulties as well as the joys of motherhood. With the ratio of divorce to marriage running so high, it makes good sense for a couple to take at least a couple of years to see if they can make it in a primary relationship before considering parenthood.

Shifting from an adult- to a child-centered relationship is a lot more drastic than shifting from singlehood to a primary relationship with another person. Men tend to believe what they tell women about the glories of motherhood, little realizing the impact a child will have on the couple relationship or how it will structure the lives of the parents for twenty years or so. Few husbands and wives come to any clear understanding of how they plan to rearrange their responsibilities to take account of the child. They do not realize that in addition to bringing a third person into their relationship, they are bringing in one who will be the major focus of attention for a long time. A child's needs must be met. What usually happens is that the wife is left with the responsibility for supplying 90 per cent of those needs. Although men seldom realize how much frustration and resentment is engendered by the childrearing process, or how stultifying it can be for their wife, they quickly learn that baby comes first and father comes second (Feldman, in Michel, 1971).

Because becoming a parent is more often a byproduct of making love than a deliberate act of creation, it is easy to overlook the awesome responsibility involved. No task is assumed by so many with so little preparation. Even a barber must be licensed and trained before we allow him to cut hair, but we allow people to have babies with less community control than we exercise over cows having calves!

Some people seem to have a special talent for childrearing and a strong desire to devote their lives to this enterprise. In the future, such people will specialize in childrearing just as people specialize in medicine, teaching, or economics. In the meantime, we at least have the means of controlling conception, so that those who feel inadequate, for whatever reason, to raise children will not be forced to do so. No doubt this will result in a greater percentage of happy, healthy, sound children, for there can be no doubt that unhappy, unhealthy, troubled children are most likely to have grown up in homes where the parents felt inadequate to cope with childrearing.

Complex living groups have fewer children per adult than two-person marriages. These groups appear to have found a middle ground in which they can enjoy both adult- and child-centered experiences. With child care spread among many adults, no one individual is responsible for the entire task. All can share the experience of parenting; and the children not only get more adult attention, but are exposed to a number of different adult models as well.

Irrespective of the decision to have children, most women expect to work for at least some part of their married life. With a career comes money, and with money comes power. Researchers have affirmed that employment increases the power of the wife (Hoffman and Nye, 1974). A housewife, totally dependent on her mate, perhaps not even knowing what his income is, is not a likely candidate for autonomy. Good jobs require educational preparation; but women still seem to be going to college to get a better man rather than to get a better job. As recently as 1972, Coleman (1974) found that although men may leave college to take jobs, women will leave right in the middle of the semester to get married. Incidentally, this is very short-sighted, since it leaves the woman in "bad standing" in addition to forfeiting all her credits for that semester. But as more women enter the workforce, and as women move into more significant jobs, more of the problems of achieving peerdom in the primary relationship will fade into insignificance. Already, 7.2 per cent of the working wives make more than their husbands. On the other hand, this fact in itself can be expected to create problems for some couples.

The woman who takes the idea of having a career seriously

(and 30 per cent of all working women already do) may find that she threatens many people. Her mother may be upset because she earns more than her brother. Adult friends may tell her she is depriving a male breadwinner of a job! If she is considering establishing a primary relationship with a man, she may be shocked to discover that he expects her to give up her job and become a housewife. The outside pressures may not be easy to take; but if women continue to give in to them, the day of shoulder-to-shoulder equality with men will never come for women in general.

Assuming the female member of a primary relationship does have control of biology and is economically self-supporting, there is still the likelihood that she will not act as though she is an autonomous person in the relationship. She must also initiate and take responsibility, not just for herself, but for the relationship, just as her male partner does. This indicates that she is also psychologically autonomous, and it is a key test of a peer relationship. Each person in the relationship—not just the male—should feel equally free to initiate within a framework of agreed-upon givens.

> Paula and Sam, after many years of marriage, gradually evolved a peer relationship that seemed well-suited to their individual needs. Their two children, both teenagers, viewed their open relationship as a very "matter of fact" given, and looked upon their intimate friends as "closer than family." When one of Paula's friends who had moved to Boston asked her to fly east for the weekend, she had no idea that he would be introducing her to a client of his who was looking for a new department head. The job involved a substantial pay increase and great responsibility, not to mention being in the same town with Ted. Paula tentatively accepted the job, and then spent the rest of the weekend gathering information about places to live, costs, schools, and all the other pertinent data she needed to take back to discuss with Sam and the children before making a firm decision.

If this illustration surprises you, try a little experiment. Assume that Ted was Sam's friend, who had asked him to come to Boston, and so forth. Does it make a difference? It shouldn't!

The quest for autonomy through personal growth in a peer relationship is somewhat different if there are more than two people in the relationship. Because more mutual growth areas can be found in a larger group, more growth occurs. In a two-person relationship, interests that are not shared usually are not developed. On the other hand, with more people in the group, one must find more private time for the assimilation of new ideas and for "keeping one's head together."

Kathy tried to help her mother understand why she and Carl were living in a group marriage with Peggy, Earl and Mike. How could this be an improvement on conventional marriage? The breakthrough came unexpectedly when she was talking about how she related to each mate. "I keep up my exercise with Peggy. She is teaching me ballet and I'm teaching her yoga. You know how Carl hates exercise! I've already taken off all those pounds! Remember how he used to try to get me to do his language bit? He and Earl are studying Russian together and they both love it. And I have Mike to discuss business with, thank goodness. I used to bore Carl to tears with economics. He just couldn't get into it. And I felt the same way about his test development work. But Peggy is fascinated by test development. It relates somehow to her mathematical models of predictive theory. We all are so excited about the years of exploring and growing together we see ahead of us. I feel like a new person."

The available evidence suggests that most people prefer the less binding ties of intimate friendship to the intensity of complex living situations. It is a lot easier to relate to one other person in a primary relationship plus a group of intimate friends than it is to have multiple primary relationships, or even to live with other people, as well as a primary mate, in the same house. Singles and couples alike can involve themselves to a greater or lesser degree at will, without making waves, when they do not live together.

Evidence from the past does not suggest that a substantial number of people will enter into complex living groups in the future. Nevertheless, some authors (Comfort, 1972; Otto, 1971; Rimmer, 1968; Roy, and Roy, 1968; Constantine and Constantine, 1970) suggest that various types of complex living groups will grow in popularity and that both these living groups and peer marriages will be supported by a very substantial growth of intimate friendship groups and networks, which will supplement and in some instances replace the kinship networks of yesteryear.

7

Intimacy,
Sex and Companionship,
or Whatever Happened to Love?

Chris and Frank have worked together for six years. When he decided to quit engineering and go into general contracting, Frank asked Chris to design his stationery and a brochure and in the process he discovered that she had a fund of information about going into business that led him to consult with her more and more often. Finally he asked her if she would handle the administration and management of his new business while he concentrated on developing sales and handling operations. As his company grew, Chris began to find it so interesting and time consuming that she sold her own printing business and became Frank's general manager. Chris and Frank spend long hours together, sometimes in the field sometimes in the office, and they are a very effective team. Frank's wife, Judy, says she and Stan, Chris's husband, both play second fiddle to Chris' and Frank's business, but she says it fondly. The four are good friends although they do not socialize together very much. When Chris is away her kids stay at Judy's; and when something at Judy's needs fixing it is usually Stan who fixes it. Frank and Chris share emotional, intellectual and career intimacy. In six years, during which they have on occasion slept in the same bed, they have not been sexually intimate. The four are family intimates, but only Judy and Stan have much social life together. On one of the rare occasions when both families were together skinny dipping with the kids in the lake on a new building site Frank had just acquired, the two couples did discuss open sexuality. They don't have anything against open sexuality, but feel that somehow they have already gone past the point of relating sexually. "We sort of take it for granted that sexual intimacy is a part of our relationship that hasn't happened yet, but probably will."

Are these four people intimate or not? As far as they are concerned, the answer is yes. Intimacy is a very subjective thing. As we indicated in Chapter Three, the degree of commitment varies with respect to the different aspects of intimate relating: social, sexual, emotional, intellectual, family and career, or work. Intimates may be very committed on some of these levels and not involved at all on others. We discovered these two couples because one of them, Judy, is an associated member of an intimate network. She still maintains an intimate relationship with a college roommate that involves a high degree of commitment on the sexual and emotional levels. Clara is the only woman Judy ever related to sexually, although she would like to relate sexually to Chris. She has never mentioned this to Chris, Frank or Stan, however, because she fears that it might somehow come between Chris and Stan or Chris and Frank, and she loves them all too much to take a chance on hurting them.

Earlier we talked about the amount of caring and sharing that changes a casual or superficial relationship into an intimate relationship. We suggested that at the heart of such a relationship one finds an ongoing dialogue, trust, and responsibility. Where most people get confused and concerned about this definition of intimacy as including sexual intimacy is with respect to the sanctity of sex. They are apt to say that sex without love is mechanical and repugnant, and that loving sex occurs only in marriage. If one probes this argument, it usually turns on two points: First, that it is against the law/religion to relate sexually outside marriage; and second, that you can't separate human sexuality from the procreative function without doing violence to the concept of love—"that's what love-making is for, ultimately," they say. We have considered this argument at length in Chapter Five in our discussion of the effect of positive and/or permanent contraception in separating clearly the love-making function from the baby-making function. Our observation of both individuals and couples in intimate groups and networks suggests very strongly that the deep bonds of love we find there are of the same type we find in marriage, although they do not extend to the degree, in most cases, where they constitute a primary relationship. In her discussion of the partial loss of personhood married people experience because of the couple-front (i.e., a couple is only invited if neither host nor hostess objects to husband or wife, so that many people are not invited because of their spouse and most marrieds will not ask only one spouse to visit), Lonny Myers (1973) points out that the institution of marriage actually covers a wide spectrum of different types of relationships and that the *only* thing they have in common is a certain legal status.

I would be willing to go further than this and suggest that the wide spectrum of *intimate relationships,* which I call INTIMATE FRIENDSHIPS, *includes* marriages and similar primary relationships somewhere along the spectrum; but that the spectrum extends beyond the primary relationship portion in both directions. It includes many degrees of intimacy that are *less* committed than a couple feels may be sufficient to constitute a primary relationship. It also includes many degrees of intimacy that are *more* committed than a primary relationship: for example, take the case of a sexually open marriage (a primary relationship plus intimate friends) or a group marriage involving multiple primary relationships and perhaps intimate friends as well.

Where, then, are the anchor points at each end of this spectrum? At the upper end, it seems clear to me that a group marriage that is sexually open tests the top limits, for such a situation involves multiple primary relationships as well as additional intimate friendships of a less than primary stature. The Roys (1970) said: "Sexual expressions should be proportional to the depth of a relationship. This leads, of course, to the conclusion that *most* [my emphasis] coitus and other intimate expressions should only occur with very close friends." The lower end of the intimate friendship spectrum occurs at that point in an otherwise traditional friendship at which the individuals involved agree that sexual intimacy is acceptable and appropriate behavior between friends. Notice that it is the *potential* for sexual intimacy that must be agreed upon, not sexual activity. Intimate friendship may never involve fulfilling the sexual potential of the relationship, but it accepts the sexual aspect of friendship, along with the emotional, intellectual, social, family, and work aspects, as a legitimate function of friendship.

But what about those individuals who bed-hop without any commitment—the swingers and others who are involved in one night stands? In the case of both singles and couples, the problem may often have to do with failure to develop sufficient positive connective tissue before sexual intimacy occurs. There appears to be a tendency for most of us to think of all the negatives in a relationship in the "cold light of dawn" the next morning after initial sexual intimacy occurs. Unless there has been sufficient effort to develop positives in the relationship to offset these negatives, especially if the sexual experience wasn't that great anyway, the chances are that the friendship will wither overnight. It is interesting to note that this is a very common occurrence in dating patterns among most unmarried individuals, not just among the so-called swinging singles. In New York City, for example, many singles believe that nobody dates more than three times without going to bed. This isn't very much time to make up your mind!

Interestingly enough, swinging couples are simply replicating the dating pattern of the unmarried, but on a couple basis. Their chances of success are even more limited, however, because they operate on a couple-front basis; thus four people must find each other agreeable, rather than two. Most swinging couples are as interested in developing lasting relationships as are the singles. In either case, however, there are some people who apparently don't want to relate on any other basis than the sexual. We hear them labeled with many pejoratives, such as "hard-core swingers." Is it any less positive to relate to others on one level of intimacy than another, however? And might not the relationship make up in intensity what it lacks in longevity? Would we condemn a couple for relating only on the social level, or the emotional level, or the intellectual level? I seriously doubt it. I suspect much of the negative labeling of relationships that involve only sexual intimacy are based on either the "Protestant Ethic" or on the theory that a one night stand with a stranger involves the avoidance of intimacy. Yet even this most minimal of involvements may, and often does, lead to the development of a lifelong relationship. How many stories have you ever heard about love at first sight? How many stories do you know about friends of yours who came together under the unlikeliest of circumstances and have been together ever since? It is easy to condemn people who are unsure of the degree to which they are willing to commit themselves when their limits are geared down to very minimal relating. Yet we all start somewhere, and any kind of start is a beginning. Lynn and Jay Smith (1975), who have interviewed many hundreds of swingers over a number of years, report that over a period of several years fifty per cent of those who started out on a couple-front basis have gradually extended their limits, relaxing them to the point of swinging on an individual basis or even to the point of evolving a sexually open relationship. This suggests quite a bit of growth over a comparatively short time. It is pretty hard to imagine a sharing of sexual intimacy, even on a one time only basis, that is completely devoid of any involvement at all.

Some people, especially males, have difficulty relating to sex in a caring, sharing, loving way. They have been socialized to see sex as competitive and performance-oriented. As teenagers they compare notes, boast about conquests, real or imagined, and often go out of their way to hide feelings of loving concern for their sexual partners from their buddies. Women are socialized to be caring and sharing and to value concern for others and feelings over performance-rating. This is one of the areas in which "male liberation" is sorely needed. Unfortunately, in the early days of women's liberation, the bra-burning declarations of independence played right into the hands of the male scalp collectors. They were quick to point out to their dates that a liberated female did as she pleased, not as tradition demanded, and often the ploy worked, and the guy was able to make a "conquest" where he otherwise would not have scored.

Before long, the situation changed, however. As women became more aggressive they began to make demands of their own, fortified by their knowledge that Masters and Johnson had declared their capacity for sex to be infinite, whereas the male capacity is very finite indeed. Armed with this new knowledge and the temptation to overreact to the years of repression and of being put down by males who were concerned only for their own pleasure, many women turned the tables on the men; and soon therapists began to report an increase in male patients with impotence problems.

The unfortunate part of this reversal is that it moves in the wrong direction—not toward more love and intimacy—but toward a "Mexican standoff" between men and women. Now there are both males and females who use sex to keep people at arm's length, rather than to relate to others and open up. Humans are never so vulnerable as immediately following orgasm. This is a major reason why many people use sexual intimacy as an avenue to establishing intimate friendships—because it is a "short cut" to making one's self vulnerable—and it is this willingness to be vulnerable to the partner that promotes the sharing of intimacy and love. It is for this reason that men are more likely than women to "want out" of swinging. The usual sequence is that the male does a little arm twisting of his wife or girlfriend to get her to try swinging with him. She is often reluctant, but goes along with the idea of pleasing him. Then when she gets involved, she often discovers that she really enjoys it; and as a result, it is the women who control swinging activities. The man may become more and more dismayed as he sees how much she enjoys this activity, whereas he may be finding the situation much more demanding than he had anticipated: He may discover that, like the kid who is told he can eat all the candy he wants, the anticipation was a lot more exciting than the reality. As it happens, the kid gets over the stomach ache a lot faster than the man gets over the bruised ego.

This may be the first step in the educational process that a man must go through if he is to overcome his aggressive, competitive socialization and graduate to the level on which the female usually starts—a level at which it is both possible and desirable to share feelings, express emotions, forget about performance, and concentrate on loving. Today, more and more young men are learning the lesson at college age and do not need to be "resocialized" later, as is the case with so many older men. These older men have not learned in their traditional marriages, because the contrast between male and female views is not so marked in the marriage bed as it is in swinging. One's wife is not likely to call attention to this performance orientation if she feels dependent and subordinate in the relationship. What about marriages in which there is no longer any sexual relating?

Some people have argued that marriage has to take on the companionate role in order to survive. They reason that sex and companionship appear to be incompatible in the same relationship, citing the facts that the divorce rate is nearly half the marriage rate, that people are not naturally monogamous, and that married sex becomes a deadly dull routine very quickly. They conclude that the only realistic expectation is adultery or serial monogamy, a polite form of polygamy in which one has several mates in a row instead of having them simultaneously. Since divorce is approaching 50 per cent of the marriage rate and adultery is practiced by a majority of married individuals, these commentators suggest that the only hope for a lasting marriage is to build a companionate relationship on the funeral pyre of the initial sexual involvement and look elsewhere for sexual intimacy. This view of the potential of a two-person primary relationship is static rather than growing, and it is unsavory as well, suggesting that one must be a sexual sneak in order to survive in marriage. It simply fails to come to grips with the possibility of a peer relationship between two open, accepting, sharing, growing individuals who have no use for adultery because they do not need to sneak off in secret either in order to share intimacy with friends or to bring that intimacy back to their primary relationship for resharing with their mate.

The experience of those in the previously mentioned intimate groups and networks study is overwhelmingly in the direction of finding their primary relationship strengthened rather than weakened by their intimate friendships outside the primary relationship. Far from diminishing their sexual interest in each other, they find that that interest increases because it is fed both by new knowledge gained outside the relationship and by the realization that the depth of sexual understanding and responsiveness they share as one component of their primary relationship makes the sexual component of their relating very special as compared to their outside sexual relationships.

In 1963, Foote wrote "the origin of friendships in connection with the development of new interests and their expiration with the arrest or decline of previous common interests, suggests that an ample supply of successive and concurrent common interests must be forthcoming to maintain the friendships of long duration. Pairs of persons who never grow tired of each other are few and far between. There is no *a priori* basis for assuming that male–female pairs who do enjoy each other indefinitely are the people who always get married to each other, [but] successful marriage can be defined in terms of its potential for continued development [rather] than in terms of momentary assessments of adjustment."

Actually, there is some evidence in research studies suggesting that companionship, like sexual interest, is highest in the early years of marriage and steadily declines until sometime in the middle years, rising again in old age, but never returning to the high level existing between a bride and groom. This decline is directly associated with childbearing and rearing, the leveling out phase beginning when the children are preschoolers. Reported positive companionship activities drop from 70 per cent at marriage to 35 per cent when the first child is a preschooler and remain in the 35–40 per cent range thereafter (Rollins and Feldman, 1970). There is no similar decline in childless marriages.

⸢In 1973, the Francoeurs stated: "An open [peer] marriage is an honest relationship between two people who accept each other as equals, friends, and partners. It is a non-manipulative, non-exploitive relationship with equal freedom and identity for both partners, allowing and encouraging each to enrich [themselves and] their primary relationship with a variety of relationships that complement and reinforce the marriage. Open marriages are custom made and highly individual. There is no single unchanging archetype, as there is for closed [traditional] marriage. Furthermore, each unique open marriage is made more unique because it is constantly growing and evolving."

In such a growing primary relationship, the caring, sharing, and helping that I would identify as love, because it involves active concern for the partner that transcends one's own need, is precisely the same kind of relationship found among intimate friends to a lesser degree. This is generally the case because, as we have already indicated, the partners tend not to let their outside involvements impinge on the time or psychic space of their primary relationship except in emergency situations. Because their outside intimate relationships are a part of their input to the primary relationship—are a shared and "savored" and accepted addition to their loving involvement with each other— the idea of jealousy becomes almost a non sequitur. Love does not occur without intimacy⸢ Intimate friendships are loving relationships in which both the needs of the individual and the desire of the individual to meet the intimate partner's needs before consideration of her/his own are paramount⸥ Intimate friends often refer to one another as lovers or otherwise indicate their love for their intimate friends.

Among those who practice peer marriage the nature of outside intimate relationships vary in intensity over time and in terms of the relative needs of the primary *and* ancillary relationships. There may be times when neither mate is currently deeply involved outside the relationship because their intimate friends are not nearby in time and space or because either one of them or one of the outside partners are involved in some other aspect of their lives that has higher priority. Thus we have found people described as intimate friends whom the individual has not seen for perhaps ten years; and we find confirmation of the still existing relationship from the other end.

It is striking to note how much ancillary intimate relationships resemble primary relationships in many cases. Outsiders often assume that the couple are married to each other because of the nonverbal communication between them; and in the earlier stages of the relationship, the parallel to lovers and newlyweds may be pronounced in a few instances. Likewise, the amount of specifically sexual involvement is likely to be higher at first and then taper off. Nevertheless, the sum total of ancillary relationships, whether one or many, should not really threaten the primary relationship because it will always be growing so much faster than they will, since it receives the bulk of the couples' attention. Thus the problem of jealousy isn't much of a problem.

As a number of respondents in the study of intimate networks have indicated, when they decided to form a primary relationship, they dropped out of the network for a while until they could consolidate their new relationship. An eighteen year old daughter of a peer couple explained that she understood, approved, and enjoyed the overflowing warmth of her parents' intimate friendships. She found it very difficult, however, to translate their open relating to where she was at the moment because she had no primary relationship already built on solid ground. Multiple relationships naturally became competing relationships, any one of which might become primary. Thus the fellows she dated had a great deal of trouble dealing with her adamant refusal to accept an exclusive relationship with any one of them. They had a reason to be jealous that simply did not exist in her parents' relationships.

As Margaret Mead said in 1960: "Jealousy is not a barometer by which the depth of love may be read. It merely records the degree of the lover's insecurity. It is a negative, miserable state of feeling, having its origin in a sense of insecurity and inferiority." [7] "The conquest of sexual jealousy, if achieved, could be the greatest advance in human relations since the advent of common law or the initiation of democratic processes" (Smith and Smith,

1974). Individuals who are considering opening up their primary relationship need to consider the very real difference between an intellectual acceptance of the concept of peer relating and the gut level ability to deal successfully with a situation in which their primary partner spends part or all of the night with somebody else. No amount of intellectualizing about it can really substitute for the moment of truth, when you are *here* and she is *there*. I say she deliberately, because it is usually the female who actually becomes involved outside the primary relationship first, although it may have been the male who initiated the idea or it may have been a joint conversation out of which the notion grew. As we indicated earlier, the conceptualization usually does not come from the female, but the initial action usually does.

Jealousy as a result of feeling left out is certainly reasonable. If your mate is in the next room, very audibly making love while you sit alone, listening, you would be a very unusual person if you did not feel left out. But if you are somewhere else, involved in some other activity, you have no more reason to feel jealous of your mate than your mate has to feel jealous of you. The kind of activity in which each of you is involved is unimportant. In fact, there can be many situations in which your mate might have greater justification to be jealous of your nonsexual activity than you have to be jealous of your mate's sexual activity.

Harvey and Sue have been married for fifteen years. Both are in the creative arts, and Sue had been involved in intimate friendships outside the marriage for about six years, up until six months ago. At that time she became so uncertain about the degree to which Harvey was really committed to peer marriage that she broke off two relationships and the sexual aspect of a third. She and Harvey spent the weekend with the friends with whom she had an incipient relationship and she attempted to get Harvey to commit himself with respect to how he felt about sexually open marriage in a four-way conversation. In six years Harvey had not acted upon the openness potential of their sexually open marriage, nor had he, to her knowledge, ever acknowledged the existence of the agreement, except in conversation with her; and she felt that if he was willing to commit himself openly with respect to the agreement, perhaps she would feel less ill at ease about it. Unfortunately, the discussion did nothing to relieve her suspicions that he was simply accommodating to her wishes because he loved her very much. When he suggested that she feel free to sleep with the other couple Saturday night, he only added to her perplexity.

Every couple has to find out for itself whether or not each partner is actually able to handle the other's outside intimate relating. If one is able to handle it and the other is not, then there will probably be no sexually open relationship until the two are able to make the one partner comfortable with such a relationship, and it is conceivable that this means never. In a supposedly sexually open relationship in which one partner never becomes intimately involved outside the primary relationship, the other partner is likely to discontinue outside relationships too, as a result of being unsure that the inactive partner is not just giving "lip-service" to the principle of peer relating without actually being committed to the idea. This may result in unfair pressure on the nonrelating partner to "make good" on the commitment.

If love were a finite thing, then jealousy might be a realistic reaction in the face of sharing love with another. But we know that love is infinite. Does a mother take 50 per cent of her love away from her husband and give it to her firstborn? What about a mother with nine kids? Do husband and children each have their shares subdivided down to 10 per cent each with the advent of the ninth child? Of course not. The capacity to love increases with the exercise of love. We have said that love involves the mutual desire to put meeting the need of the other in an intimate relationship before having our own need met. We have also seen that the degree of intimate involvement may vary greatly with respect to the social, sexual, intellectual, emotional, family, and work vectors of the intimate relationship. In our example at the beginning of this chapter, Judy may well have more reason to be jealous of Chris and Frank's work intimacy than Frank has to be jealous of her sexual and emotional relationship with Clara.

In actual fact, jealousy wouldn't make any sense in either case. Each of these relationships serves a function that is complimentary to Judy and Frank's primary relationship. Frank is grateful to Clara for providing a kind of emotional sharing for Judy that is different than the emotional relationship in their marriage but is still very important to Judy. He and Clara are fast friends because they share love for Judy, and, consequently, concern, respect, and warmth for each other.

As Valentine Michael Smith said (Heinlein, 1961): "The joining of bodies with merging of souls in shared ecstasy, giving, receiving, delighting in each other . . . is the source of all that makes this planet so rich and wonderful. And until a person has enjoyed this treasure bathed in the mutual bliss of minds linked as closely as bodies [he has not been intimate]." Love is still doing very well, thank you.

8

Ground Rules for Relating: Maximizing Pleasure While Minimizing Problems

Every individual has an internalized set of ground rules for relating to others, whether s/he knows it or not. For many of us it is during early adolescence that we begin to be concerned about our own brand of values. Up until that time we have been socialized by home, school, peers, church, and others but we have not usually thought much about what *we* think is right or wrong. Once such thoughts occur, and we build a consciously considered value set, we then proceed to measure peers and others, but especially parents, by these rules, to see if they "measure up."

All value sets are *subjective*. Standards of honesty, truth, fidelity, and bravery, are all projections of particular groups, rather than universal norms. Honesty is one thing in one time and place, something else in another. We call this "situational ethics." It is hard to remember that values are not universally the same because we automatically project our own particular value set onto all that we see or read or hear. Thus it is very difficult to *really* communicate because the value words we use mean something different to different people, and the more divergent their background in time and place, the more differences of meaning there are likely to be. A few examples will illustrate what I mean. Laughter is an expression of extreme embarrassment for the Japanese. In some groups belching at the table is a compliment to the hostess—failure to belch is an insult. In some situations it is not polite to tell the truth. We frequently tell people things that are not so because we do not wish to hurt them or offend them or because what we are saying is what we think they want to hear. Part of the process of social mobility involves learning a new and different set of values to exchange for the old set. In our geographically mobile society, we also have to relearn the local interpretation of value sets each time we move. The trouble is that because we all use the same terms to describe what may be quite different values, we constantly get in trouble without realizing it. What are the implications of these illustrations for intimate relationships?

During the process of forming intimate relationships, it is extremely important for individuals to try to develop some mutual understanding of each other's value sets because each is interested in correctly assessing the other's behavior. Each tries to learn something of the other's background, and to discuss issues that relate to her/his own ground rules for relating, in order to determine whether or not there is sufficient common meeting ground for continuing to build a relationship. Unfortunately, not too many people discuss their ground rules directly because they may not be aware of them or because they may not wish to reveal them. In fact, in America, many people feel that it is good, rather than bad (appropriate rather than inappropriate), to avoid exposing their ground rules for relating. They may do this in order not to risk hurting the other person, or perhaps because they are afraid of giving the other an advantage if they reveal too much about their decision-making process.

A man may avoid revealing his age, for example, because he suspects the woman he is interested in will lose interest in him if she learns that he is six years younger than she. A woman may hide her Ph.D. until she is sure this will not frighten a man off. A man may not reveal that he is only interested in aggressive women, or Jewish women, or "old family" women, or women who share his desire to have six children.

It is sad, but true, that many people actually make a deliberate effort to avoid thinking about these bases for relating. They like to think that they are free and objective and open to any love relationship because they have the notion that it is somehow underhanded or unloving to make *conscious* decisions about relating. It is part of the romantic ideal that such conscious decisions are heavy-handed, self-serving, calculating and probably doomed to failure anyway. After all, doesn't the poor but sweet guy marry the factory owner's daughter in the end? As a matter of fact, no, he doesn't, usually. Marriage choices tend to be made within the parameters of age, social class, education, religion, propinquity, race, and ethnic group. People select mates of similar social, psychological and physical makeup.

We have found that individuals in the intimate groups and networks we studied used the same approach to develop either intimate friendships or primary relationships, regardless of whether they were currently married or single and in a primary relationship or not. Each sought to develop relationships within a framework of trust, honesty, openness, acceptance of change, willingness to work toward consensus, and the realization that the odds were against developing such a relationship. The failure rate is high for peer relating because those who look for such relationships set high standards. Once established, however, their survival rate is excellent. This is in marked contrast to the traditional pattern of relating, and it scares off most people in a hurry. Many people do not like to talk about what they are doing, nor do they wish to be honest and open and above board about their motives.

Glenna leveled with Jerry on their first date. She told him that she was not interested in being anybody's flunkie or "girl" and that she was and would remain her own person in any relationship she formed. She indicated her lack of interest in getting married, her dedication to her career, and her determination to find a guy who could share without taking over. She said she was looking for a man who was good in bed, but willing to build a nonexclusive relationship on a partnership basis. Jerry left early and she never saw him again.

Glenna wasn't bothered. She feels that her "trauma" approach saves her a lot of "weeding out" time.

Once the possibility of relating survives the initial screening process for both parties, a second phase of relating begins in which the individuals must develop ground rules for their relationship. First, however, they must evolve the process for rule-making. As we indicated earlier, communication *always* involves setting rules for interaction and verifying or challenging either dominance or parity in the relationship; and in most cases, this interaction is largely nonverbal. A person who wishes to establish a peer relationship strives to make this process verbal or at least to reinforce the nonverbal communication verbally.

The person who dominates interaction will in all likelihood set the rules for relating. In a traditional relationship, the first few months are often a shattering experience for each partner as each learns how different the other's expectations were. This is especially true for the woman because she has relinquished the rule-making to the man. Now she is faced with operating by his rules, and the changes slip up on her before she realizes what is happening.

Fred moved into Ellen's apartment a couple of months after they began seeing each other. At his place they had both shared the cooking chores but at her place she cooks. Ellen suddenly realizes her position one evening after Fred has been living with her for a couple of weeks when she arrives home from work a few minutes before he does and sits down to read the mail. When he arrives, Fred asks, "How soon do we eat?" The question assumes her responsibility to provide a meal and Ellen's response is to feel guilty because she didn't start dinner before reading the mail. The implied negative judgment is one of guilt by default, because she never challenged Fred's authority to make the rules. For Ellen, it is not too late to change things if she really wants to. Had she and Fred married before moving in together, things would have been a lot more complicated at this juncture. The "trapped" feeling would be much more pronounced, and the potential embarrassment in breaking up would be an important factor in Fred's ability to get her to "knuckle under."

Our concern, however, is not with traditional relationships, but with peer relating. A peer relationship is vastly different conceptually than a traditional one. It exists only for as long as each partner continues to feel that there is more to be gained by staying in the relationship than by getting out; and if the partners do not continue to be peers, then there is no point in continuing the relationship. Thus a traditional marriage can exist as an empty shell—form without substance—as described by Cuber and Harroff in their famous study of the upper-middle class marriage. But peer marriage is process oriented—it exists for the purpose of permitting and promoting the growth of the partners, as well as the growth of their relationship together. They have entered into the relationship because each believes that together they can each grow faster and further and more joyously than if they "go it alone." This is why the Francoeurs' definition of peer marriage stressed the continuing uniqueness of each such relationship. Each partner must assume responsibility for what he puts into the relationship, for self-growth, and for maintaining the viability of the peer-bond. Otherwise it will either break up or slide back into the traditional mold.

If the individual retains responsibility/control with respect to his or her own growth and intimacy, then the focus of the relationship is clearly on process rather than on content, and it is in this area that the difference between a pair-bond and a peer-bond is really pronounced. It is quite possible for a traditional marriage to continue to exist even though it is only a vehicle of convenience for the people in it. Our laws say that fidelity is a contractual component of the relationship rather than a personal matter. But fidelity cannot be legislated, and in a legal sense it has come to mean that a married person should restrict all aspects of intimacy to the marriage.

In a peer relationship, however, fidelity to the relationship does not restrict intimacy. Rather, fidelity is measurable in terms of the degree to which the partners have actually succeeded in permitting and promoting the growth of each person as well as of the relationship between them. Infidelity thus is failure to meet the responsibility for structure, norms, and consequences of the peer-bond rather than the establishment of additional intimate relationships outside the peer-bond. At the heart of any primary relationship is the expectation that members will give the primary relationship their primary loyalty. As we have said before, this means protecting the primary relationship's time and psychic space vis-à-vis other relationships. Just as it was important for the individual to be self-protective in setting up the primary relationship, so it is important for each partner to protect the peer-bond.

What kinds of ground rules do couples in peer-bond relationships develop to protect their primary relationship vis-à-vis the intimate friendships of each partner? In the intimate groups and networks study we found 255 married individuals and another 54 who were living in primary relationships not involving marriage, a total of 309, or 81 per cent of the total sample of 380 individuals.

GROUND RULES FOR HANDLING OUTSIDE INTIMATE RELATIONSHIPS

The following ten ground rules were used by these people to protect their primary relationships.

Be extremely wary of potential intimate friends who are looking for a new primary relationship, or are in therapy, marriage crisis, or other highly unsettled personal situation. Fifty-nine per cent of the sample felt the necessity to be very cautious about pursuing a new relationship that could be expected to be very time consuming, emotionally draining, and a possible direct challenge to their own peer-bond. Many indicated that they had learned the hard way that getting involved in someone else's problem situation could very quickly become a "sticky wicket" and that once having had the experience, they and their primary partner became sensitized to this possibility and engaged in protracted dialogue whenever one of them felt that a potential new relationship might get them involved in similar difficulties. The focus here is on *potential* relationships, not on ongoing relationships. Once the intimate friendship exists, the willingness to rally to the help of a friend in crisis is one of the distinguishing features of intimate friendships.

Family obligations come first. Forty-three per cent of the sample made a point of putting family obligations ahead of intimate friendship. An alternative favored by many was the trading off of family obligations with their primary partner so that only an emergency situation would raise such an issue.

The sum of all outside relationships is not allowed to impinge on the time or psychic territory of the primary relationship. Forty per cent of the sample have such a rule. It is sometimes expressed in terms of each partner having a veto power over the other's relationships, that is, if one's mate is especially threatened or uncomfortable about an incipient relationship, one is not likely to pursue the matter further. Sometimes it is simply a matter of one partner expressing discomfort at the level or amount of the other's outside activity. Usually, however, partners are very sensitive to the need to pace themselves and their relationships in a manner that will keep them a positive factor in the primary relationship.

It is a "turn-on" to discuss potential relationships beforehand. Twenty-eight per cent of the sample indicated that they always discussed any potential relationships at length before becoming involved because they enjoyed sharing the anticipation of a new relationship and weighing the advantages and disadvantages, not just from a self-protective point of view, but because it was a way of sharing the excitement of a new adventure.

We discuss problem or potential problem situations only. Twenty-six per cent of the sample indicated no prior discussion except of potential problems. For these individuals the need to consult is reserved for a situation that is causing difficulty for the partner in the outside relationship or for one that appears to be about to cause difficulty.

One must inform one's primary partner before entering an intimate relationship, if possible, in order to provide veto opportunity. Twenty per cent of the sample individuals have a policy of prior discussion whenever possible. They recognize that this is not always feasible, but in the main, they attempt to give their mate the opportunity to express feelings about the potential relationship before it begins.

No conditions. Twenty per cent of the sample indicated that individual freedom was more important than protecting the relationship; and that there were, therefore, no conditions attached to outside intimate friendships—just as there were no conditions on education, or career choice, or any other aspect of personhood. These individuals made the point that their primary relationship must be able to cope with them as they are, that the commitment to each other, that is, of loyalty to the relationship, could not take precedence to loyalty to one's self, that is, personal integrity. Most, but not all, of these individuals were singles living in primary relationships. The issue of freedom versus commitment is at the heart of all intimate relationships. In this particular sample, therefore, 63 put freedom first, and the other 246 put commitment first.

Accept the premise that sometimes an outside relationship will impinge on the primary relationship time frame: this is not catastrophic, but is akin to the similar incursions of career and children. Fourteen per cent of the sample subscribe to this philosophy. They arrange their lives around each other's outside relationships in exactly the same way that they arrange them around all the other activities of the week. In a way, they seem less intense or concerned about whether or not they are too involved. Life is the way it is, and that's that, as far as they are concerned. People with this kind of ground rule appear to share families somewhat more than is average; and they are more likely to be in the child-centered stage of life. An intimate friend may take another's children in for a week while the other is in New York City for a week on the town.

Uninvolved third parties must be protected first, because they are not in a position to protect themselves. Ten per cent of the sample sees to it that uninvolved mates will not be hurt by a relationship, if indeed it comes to a question of who gets hurt, the intimate friends or their mates. This ground rule has to do with establishing intimate friendships. If an individual considers getting involved with someone who is currently in a primary relationship, it is important that s/he ascertain whether or not it is a sexually open relationship, and if not, what the consequences of establishing the intimate friendship are likely to be for the friend's primary partner. This becomes *the* or at least *a* governing factor in the decision to become involved. This is an extension of the same consideration the individuals would give to their own partners, if they are also in primary relationships. Some individuals pursue this question to the point of open discussion with the third party, if circumstances permit.

One must leave others at least as well off as one found them. Nine per cent of the sample indicated a strong sense of responsibility for the person with whom they develop an intimate friendship. John, who had a very strong peer-bond relationship, was quite attracted to Gloria, and she to him; but he worried about the fact that she had been divorced from an alcoholic husband for eleven years and during that time had done very little dating. He was concerned that she get back into the mainstream of life; but he was also afraid that she might develop such a strong attachment to him that she would be hurt by it. He talked this potential problem over with his wife and with Gloria and they all three felt that it would be all right to proceed—with caution. John and Gloria had an electrifying effect on each other. Soon she was dating other men, and within six weeks she received two marriage proposals. They continued to discuss how the relationship was affecting her; and when she began turning down dates with other men, they both realized that the warning signals were up. They broke off their relationship, but on a gradual basis, and Gloria began seeing other men more often. After another six weeks the relationship ended, with an agreement that if and when Gloria developed a solid primary relationship, it might be possible for them to renew their intimate friendship.

This example illustrates a very important factor in developing and maintaining healthy intimate friendships—the importance of talking through what is going on with *all* the partners in one's relationships. We have already mentioned this point in connection with the individual who is not in a primary relationship, and with one's responsibility to discuss all relationships with one's primary partner. It is equally important to maintain this kind of openness with other intimate friends as well. The feedback function that we discussed in Chapter Four when we were talking about the way in which interaction promotes the synergistic growth of the primary relationship through both positive and negative feedback works equally well in other intimate relationships. This is the other side of "leaving people at least as well off as you found them." The end result is growth for the outside relationships as well as for the primary relationship. Consequently, there is almost a vibrant quality about some of the intimate groups we have had the opportunity to interview. They share an invigorating, alive, sense of their mutual growth that permeates the relationships with a feeling that all concerned are living life to its fullest.

At the same time, of course, intimate friends become involved in the same problems, heartaches, growing pains, and difficulties that are always associated with growth, and especially with trying to maintain multiple relationships. If a two-person relationship is difficult to keep on an even keel, a relationship involving three or four or more, even though only two are peer-bonded, is astonishingly more difficult. Apparently, however, the rewards justify the difficulties, or there would be no sexually open relationships. Because of these very difficulties, few people venture beyond peer relationships that include intimate friends outside the relationship to the more rarified area of multiple primary relationships. When it does happen, it usually just seems to slip up on the individuals involved, in much the same way as an initial primary relationship may slip up on one.

Some social scientists feel that it is impossible to maintain two or more primary relationships simultaneously. They insist that one is always more primary than the other, and that in fact where there seem to be two, one is probably in the process of being replaced by the other. Nevertheless, group marriages involving multiple primary relationships have flourished for centuries. Recently I talked to the thirty-five-year-old son of a group marriage who stoutly maintained that all members of the group have had multiple primary relationships, at least for the thirty-odd years that he can remember.

People in primary relationships generally want to live together; and complex living arrangements, with or without multiple primary relating, introduces a set of problems that are new to most people. In such settings, however, these complex living problems are overlaid with another set of problems of a structural nature. We have all been socialized to know how to function in dyadic, or two-person marriage, but we have to examine structure and process problems anew in setting up a complex group. Each group has to develop its own norms, standards, and activities, based on the expectations, needs, and background of the participants. Among the problems to be worked through will be decision-making procedures, goals, ground rules, prohibitions, intra- and extra-group sexual norms, privacy, division of labor, roles, careers, relationships with outsiders, degree of visibility, legal jeopardy, dissolution of the group, personal responsibilities outside the group (i.e., child support payments), urban or rural setting, type of shelter, geographic location, children, child-rearing practices, taxes, pooling assets, income, legal structure, education, trial period, and so forth.

In spite of the complexity of this process of setting up a complex living group or a group marriage, each of which must work through these decision areas, the track record of complex living groups is good. In the United States today there are several times as many complex living groups as there were in the sixties, when the mass media was having a field day discussing the "hippie communes." While the turnover rate is high for the drop-out, do-your-own-thing complex living group, it is much lower for the highly structured group. There are many complex living groups with more than a decade under their belts, and some have survived for two or three generations. As for group marriages, their average life may well be only slightly less than the life of a dyadic marriage. We do know fifty-six per cent of those in the Constantine study survived less than one year.

However, the same is true of one out of three dyadic marriages that end in divorce (half survive two years). Information is still so fragmentary that it is difficult to make more than an educated guess about this. The national average for the life of a marriage that ends in divorce is slightly less than seven years (Census Bureau). The Constantines (1973) reported several group marriages with a four or five year life span which were still going strong. My own research has uncovered at least one group marriage with a 37-year life span as well as evidence that many long-term group marriages exist. The participants, however, were unwilling to talk to researchers. In any event, it is safe to say that the likelihood of failure is greatest at the beginning, and that the longer a group marriage survives, the better its chances for continued survival. The Constantines' book, *Group Marriage*, is *must* reading for anyone contemplating setting up a group marriage.

Perhaps the single most important ground rule for relating is a personal one. It is the importance of reserving time and privacy for one's self in order to facilitate assimilation, integration, and evaluation of the flood of input to one's sensory systems. What we have talked about so far in this chapter had to do with relating to others. Now we need to consider the importance of relating to one's self. The two are so inextricably interactive and interdependent that it seemed appropriate to make an issue of the need for private time by talking about it separately, at the end of the chapter.

It is easy to lose one's self in the hustle and bustle of involvement in a number of exciting and rewarding relationships; but in order to appreciate what is happening to you it is necessary to get your head together now and then, to re-examine who you are and where you stand. Just as it is necessary to open up to change and growth potential, it is also necessary to process what has happened, to winnow out that which is real, vital, and important to you, and to discard that which you do not need. Growth does not occur without evaluation and integration with one's previous fund of knowledge and experience. If the perceptions come too fast to be assimilated, many of them are simply lost.

An old joke among public school superintendents is to question whether a person has had twenty years experience or one year's experience twenty times. The difference is vital to those who wish to develop and maintain peer relationships. As we have noted before, a peer relationship is process oriented. *It exists only for as long as the partners continue to grow.* Nature abhors a vacuum, and so does a peer relationship. Therefore it is not enough simply to exist, to be active in the relationship, to soak up new experiences.

With growth comes pain, and sometimes it is tempting to use the need for a time for private thinking as an excuse for running away from the complexities of the interpersonal growth process instead of working them out in the dialogue with one's intimate friendship and/or primary relationship partner(s). It is important to let your partner know when you are overloaded with problems and feeling the need to hide. Try to arrive at an understanding, before there is need for it, that either or any partner can call "time out" and have his/her wishes respected without question. We all have occasions when we've "had it up to here" and can't take any more. Each must be willing to respect the other's need for respite and postpone the discussion until the "system overload" is reduced. Sometimes it is helpful to find out why the other person is in distress. In such a case, it may be possible to reduce the distress; but at other times, talking about it may add to the distress, and the better course is to exhibit the kind of loving acceptance of the other's need that one would want to receive if the roles were reversed.

9

Economics and Career:
Some Pros and Cons
of Working Together

Nora was determined to complete her education through graduate school, but money was a big problem. Her parents were willing
to help her through a B.A.; but with two brothers in the family, she
had to do a big share, too, and she knew that she would have to
manage grad school alone. Nora, like many women, was afraid to
take a student loan because she felt that it would interfere with her
chances of getting married or that it would be unfair to a future
husband. After graduating from college, she applied to several
graduate schools hoping that she could get student aid, but without
success. She would have preferred to stay at home while she worked
to earn money for grad school, but her parents' attitude was so down
on graduate education for women that she decided against doing so.
They felt that she would ruin her chance for marriage if she got any
more education, and this played on fears she already had about
career and marriage.

Immediately Nora faced a problem. With an entry-level job, she
was going to need every dollar just to make ends meet; it would be
impossible to save for grad school. She began asking around about
possible roommates to share expenses; and on impulse, she called a
friend in Lincoln, where she wanted to go to school. This friend told
her about a group of people in town with whom she should get in

touch. Nora called and was invited to come to Lincoln and talk over her situation. She found there a group of six people, two couples and two fellows, ranging in age from 30 to 45, living together in a large house. Everybody in the group was employed, two of them at the University, and they shared expenses on the basis of a full share for each adult and a ⅔ share for each of the two children. She was amazed to learn that by living with them she probably could afford to enroll in grad school immediately, because her monthly expenses would be only about half of what she had expected if she lived alone.

Banding together for economic reasons is a frequent occurrence for some groups in our society, especially for those who are just getting started or still in college, for the elderly, and among poor or working class families who take in roomers to make ends meet. In many ethnic minorities the same type of support is extended to kinfolk who live together in extended families; and in all walks of life it is not unusual for parents to provide a home for grown children, single or married, during times of need. Our concern, however, is with complex living groups rather than with relatives.

We began this book with the thesis that the individual, rather than the family, is the basic building block of society today. Paradoxically, many of the same forces in our society and economy that make it possible for the individual to operate a self-contained household also make households of three or more adults more desirable.

The sheer inconvenience of maintaining a household can be reduced dramatically by the addition of another person to share the load, thus freeing each member of the group to do more of the things that matter to him/her individually. The addition of another income has a similar effect on disposable income for all members of the group. The various changes in lifestyle that we have been discussing, such as putting off marriage until later in life, putting off childbearing until one is older, having fewer children, having no children, completing college, going to graduate school, can in part be traced to economic pressures as well as to the change in female expectations with respect to career.

Complex living groups often characterize their lifestyle as "not dropping out, but optimizing their ability to compete *within* the system." Others speak of "getting together in order to do better what we were already doing well." These people are demonstrating their ability to adapt to change, to adjust their lifestyle to an increasingly complex society. In a world in which the individual is more and more treated as a "unit," they find companionship and support in a group that goes far beyond that available in a two-person relationship. In a world in which inflation, like death and taxes, appears to be inevitable, they find, in the complex living group, a way to "have their cake and eat it too." (See Melville, 1972, for contrasting *Communes in the Counter Culture*.)

Group members are in a better position to continue or complete educational goals because the group can help them afford it. All can enjoy children; but with fewer children per capita, there is less individual sacrifice to childbearing/rearing. Each individual becomes less dependent on his/her current job or career. This makes it possible, for example, to accept a job in a different career line at a lower salary without penalizing the family standard of living, or to turn down a promotion that will involve additional sacrifice of personal time, or to refuse to be moved out of town, away from friends and preferred location, because one can afford to take the time needed to find a comparable local job.

If the group is one that pools assets and income, as in most group marriages, there is the additional advantage of trading off time for money. Everybody has an optimum level for basic expenses, beyond which excess income will be put into savings or investments. One can only eat so much; the utility bill can only go as high as leaving all the lights on 24 hours a day will cost; and one can find a similar leveling-off point for most expenses. Once normal operating expenses are being adequately covered and once a comfortable amount is in the savings account with money still left over, one either spends the excess on luxury items, such as boats, country homes, or a cottage on the shore, or one puts it into investments.

Investing wisely takes a great deal of thought and time and

one soon realizes that the process is a burden, because the time spent on this task is subtracted directly from personal time. When an individual or a couple reaches this point they either begin to give up more and more personal time, that is, the money takes over their personal lives, or they try to find someone they can trust to manage their investments professionally (which is difficult unless they have a great deal to invest), or they begin to think about the possibility of trading off money for time. Not too many people seem to take this last course, but the number is growing. If taking a promotion will increase income, increase taxes, increase the burden of investment decisions, *and* increase responsibility and time spent on the job, why take the promotion?

Those who are fortunate enough to be self-employed professionals can take direct steps to trade off money for time, either by cutting down on the number of clients they handle or the number of hours they work. Sometimes it is possible for people in other careers to do the same thing by limiting overtime or promotions or making an arrangement of some sort with their employer that has the effect of cutting hours.

People who live in a group marriage can deal with this problem in a different way. First of all, with three or more working adults in a group, pooled income will push into the luxury/investment level much sooner than it will for a couple. In groups of which we are aware, the income approximates $15,000 per adult, and for some groups it is considerably higher than this. This means that the group can afford to delegate the task of handling investments to one member of the group instead of everybody doing it; and if the burden becomes too great, this task could become a full time job. This person might well be the group manager and take responsibility for all financial matters within the guidelines approved by the group.

Another alternative is for the group to make possible shifts in personal goals. George can quit his job and go to law school, as he always wanted to. Sandy can quit being a buyer and open her own boutique. Excess income is thus traded off directly for desired lifestyle changes. In one group, a couple, Terry and Jane, reversed roles, something they had wanted to do for a long time. Terry quit his job after Jane finished graduate work in anesthesiology, and became house husband for the group. Jane, who had given up her nursing career to become a mother/housewife, was able, with her new specialty as a nurse-anesthetist, to command a salary only a few thousand a year smaller than Terry's, which the group could well afford.

In addition to these noneconomic spinoffs from pooled income, there are others. In one study (Ramey, 1972c), five problems seemed to carry special concern for couples interested in joining complex living groups. *For the wives,* the basic issues were the sense of isolation that comes from raising children, overdependence on the husband for adult contact, and less than optimal development and use of their talents and training. A complex living group can go a long way toward relieving these problems. Aside from providing multiple adult models for the children and relieving the mother of the strain of constant child care responsibilities, it also provides her with frequent opportunities to "recharge her battery" through daily contact with a variety of other adults. Perhaps even more importantly, it may make the difference between deciding to have children or not in the first place; for if the group is available for support, a woman is more likely to break into her career for the purpose of having children, knowing that she can pick up her career again much sooner than would be the case in a two-person group.

Some of the women who complained about less than optimal use of their talents weren't mothers at all. They were career women who had been forced to move at the wrong time and/or to the wrong place because of job opportunities for their husbands. A few complex living groups actually came into being precisely *because* one man in a closely knit intimate friendship group was faced with a corporate transfer, often involving a promotion as well. Sometimes groups take the kind of action that occurred in Atlanta, where one member asked Kevin how much it took for him and June to live on per month. He said he wasn't sure, but June was able to provide a concise answer—$1,200 per month. Jack then wondered out loud if it would be worth $200 each per month to the other six members of the group to keep June and Kevin in Atlanta until he could find a comparable job there. Over a period of three days the group came to the conclusion that they could and would be able and willing to ante up $200 per month each for at least five months, which Kevin estimated as the maximum time it would take him to find a comparable job. In the meantime, Kevin's boss got wind of the fact that Kevin was seriously considering leaving the firm rather than leaving Atlanta; and the day after the group made their decision, Kevin's boss called him in and offered him a comparable promotion to the one involving the move to Oshkosh, but without leaving Atlanta.

However, even though things worked out so that the group did not have to support Kevin and June, who, like most of the group, lived right up to the last penny each month and had no savings to fall back on, this experience started them thinking for the first time about how much they meant to each other and about the possibility of actually moving in together in order to achieve economies of scale.

The two issues facing the men were the need to find a means of freeing themselves from the rat race and financial insecurity, and the desire to provide their families with a higher standard of living. Both of these matters were involved in the decision of the Atlanta group to buy a small apartment complex together and move into it as vacancies arose. Three of the eight members decided against becoming involved in this project but remained intimate friends. Within a year this group was enjoying several economic advantages, such as bulk food purchasing, group insurance, and the elimination of four automobiles, in addition to lower housing costs, and the buildup of equity in their joint enterprise.

The job change problem vis-à-vis dual-career couples may be helped by the extra degree of geographic stability possible with a complex living group; but the "major breadwinner" problem gets worse in some groups. A male is very likely to feel threatened if his wife earns more than he does. Some women have turned down promotions or in other ways sought to avoid salary competition with their mates. In a complex living group this difference in incomes must be faced directly, because everyone is likely to be earning a different salary.

Some groups use the same tactics employed by a few couples to avoid this problem. They keep separate bank accounts and pool expenses. At income tax time they must then forego the possible advantage of filing a joint return in order to avoid comparing incomes. Although this seems a little far-fetched, some people actually do it. In one complex living group with such an arrangement, one couple left the group because they felt unable to "keep up" with the rest. Whenever someone bought something for the house, they felt uneasy because they could not afford to make an equivalent purchase. One of the other members of the group pointed out that since she lived in the house, she was damn well going to be comfortable in it, and to avoid doing so simply because someone else could not afford to was to give in to that person's peculiar twist on "dog in the manger" logic. Most groups simply recognize that "worth" is not measurable in dollars, and that pooling income is the only sensible way to operate, regardless of how much or how little anyone is paid.

Some couples have experimented with the idea of sharing the same job, with each having full responsibility but deciding between themselves who will cover the job when. The co-editors of a major American magazine were such a husband-wife team about fifteen years ago. In Norway, there is a small scale semiofficial conjugal work-sharing family pattern in operation: The wife-mother and husband-father work only half time, with their work hours synchronized so that one spouse will be off work while the other is at work, but not necessarily at the same job (Gronseth, 1972). Alice Rossi (1974) has suggested another alternative. She urges women to seek high level jobs because in such jobs the measure of success is getting the job done rather than putting in a set number of hours. No one questions when such a person does the work, as long as it meets quality standards, whereas a lower level job requires physical presence during certain hours.

Complex living groups have available to them a number of

legal formats that facilitate their advantageous position as compared to individuals or couples living and operating separately (Goldstein, 1974). The Atlanta group, for example, formed a corporation to buy the garden apartment complex in which they live, and they found that this made a lot of other things easier for them. It was easier for the corporation to obtain a mortgage. The corporation can pay for services to the group by members. The corporation can insure members so they have group health, accident, and life insurance as well as one insurance policy covering the property, their automobiles, and liability. Each member is personally protected against suits, damages, or the collapse of the corporation involving them in the corporation's debts. It also acts as a shield in other ways. The corporation also has a pension program for the members.

Another group might choose to use a nonprofit corporate format, a trust structure, or a partnership. One group that runs its own printing business is incorporated as a tax option, or Sub-Chapter S Corporation (under Internal Revenue Code Section 1371–1377; Reg. §§ 1.1371-1–1.1377-3.) which allows the members to be taxed as individuals rather than being subjected to corporate taxes, too, while still enjoying the protection of corporate structure. Some groups use short-term trusts for the education of their children. Others use the cooperative structure or the condominium as a vehicle for their group.

If this all sounds complex, it is. Group living really is a complex thing, emotionally, socially, economically, and legally. There can be real legal jeopardy involved in a complex living arrangement, even if you live in a state with "consenting adults" laws. The group is always at the mercy of the local establishment. They can be charged with open lewdness, running a bawdy house, failing to meet zoning or health code requirements, and if there are children, with contributing to the delinquency of a minor (See Weisberg, 1975).

In actuality, the likelihood of being hounded by the law depends more on public image than anything else. The house at 122 Elm Street looks like a disaster area. The lawn is unkempt, there is a VW bus in the driveway with flowers painted all over it, the males all have bushy beards, everybody goes barefoot or in sandals, there are no curtains on some of the windows, there is no attempt to cut the grass or pick up the garbage scattered around, and acid rock blares forth from the house far into the night. In the quiet residential neighborhood of Elm Street the complex living group at 122 is begging for trouble with the authorities.

Down in the next block, at 252 Elm Street, is another house of about the same size. It is immaculate. The neighbors see four men leave each morning, accompanied by three women, all dressed for business. Three drive away in the late model sedan, two in the sportscar, and one in a neighborhood car pool, leaving the station wagon in the driveway. On Thursdays, the car pool uses the station wagon. It would never occur to anybody on Elm Street that the people at 252 were anything but good neighbors, certainly not that they were a commune. Those among the neighbors who know better are completely unconcerned. "As long as they have respect for the neighborhood and don't make trouble, who cares what they do," one neighbor stated. "They're good customers," says the corner butcher. "They pay their bills on time."

This group is unlikely to ever come to the attention of the authorities; and if it does, it can count on the neighbors to rally to its defense. Visibility and viability are two sides of the same coin, for complex living groups. A steady stream of tourists and visitors, especially if it includes runaways and people looking for a place to "crash," calls attention to a group as surely as does an unkempt house, yard, and people. Neighbors are interested in appearances, not in substance. Acceptance is largely a matter of appearance. Groups that don't make waves have a much better chance of avoiding problems with officialdom.

When problems do arise, it is wise for the group to hire the very best legal firm they can afford. If at all possible, this firm should have been selected and used for group legal work right from the beginning, before any difficulties arise with the authorities. A phone call from a top legal firm works wonders with the bureaucracy. It immediately puts you in a whole different category, and as a group, you can afford this leverage.

A Look
at the Future

We are living in the midst of one of the most profound biological, technical, and sexual revolutions in recorded history. For those in their thirties and forties it is a very difficult time. Unlike those either older or younger, they have a foot planted firmly in both worlds, and it is very difficult for them to let go of the old ways and the old interpretations of how the world is, and wholeheartedly embrace the new and breathtaking conceptualization of human potential. We have considered a number of these reinterpretations, such as the recognition that change and conflict, rather than equilibrium, are the constants in society and in relationships between individuals; that the individual, rather than the family, is the basic building block of society; that democratic pluralism in lifestyle choices is indeed possible whether one is in a primary relationship or not; and that the clock cannot be turned back. The pill exists. Women's liberation exists. The sexual revolution is happening all around us. Instantaneous communication techniques are spreading social change like wildfire.

This section will take a look at where we seem to be going. We will explore the possible outcomes of various trends that look as though they will continue or that appear to be developing, considering their impact on the individual, on the family, on business, on government, and on our social institutions.

10

Trend Setting: Increasingly Visible Changes in Intimacy Style

The profound changes that are occurring around us spring largely from the upper-middle class. Because this is the group with the hand on the throttle, so to speak, the changeover is occurring very quickly. We spoke earlier about "trickle-down" of ideas, attitudes, and behaviors from the upper-middle class to the rest of our society. The impact of this group is much greater than is apparent in terms of trickle-down. It is the upper-middle class professionals, managers, academics, and creative people who mold public opinion, who communicate those opinions, who write them into law, and who build them into the bureaucratic structure of our human service delivery systems, such as employment, housing, health care, welfare, criminal justice, and the like. They are largely in control of the mass media, television, radio, the press, publishing, and the film industry. They control business, government, and the human service delivery systems, and they operate our colleges and universities. Thus they are in a position to make vast changes in a relatively short time.

The only new factor in this situation is the speed with which it is possible to effect change. When the Freudian sexual revolution overthrew the Victorian view of human sexuality, it took this group approximately thirty years to accomplish the change. Today, with instantaneous mass media reflecting upper-middle class views in every home in America every day, it will not take nearly so long to accomplish the new reinterpretation of the facts of life. The current revolution in how we perceive ourselves dates to the mid-1960s, beginning with the first widespread acceptance of the pill, the rise of women's liberation, the civil rights movement, the break with absolutism in the Church, and the increasing willingness by the mass media to talk about change.

The upper-middle class always superimposes its standards on the rest of society, proclaiming them to be the natural order of nature, the moral framework of history, and the rational approach to life. Never mind that the current frame of reference may be newly minted. The ideal lifestyle of the moment is quickly institutionalized by supportive legal regulations, by public school and higher education textbooks, by the press and the media, by use in advertising, by incorporation in the set of assumptions by which human service professionals practice their professions, and by the decisions made by business.

The Freudian sexual revolution dealt not just with an interpretation of human sexuality, but with an entire world view based on that interpretation, involving a reinterpretation of childrearing practices, courting behavior, division of the population into the normal and the "sick," labeling criminal behavior, and so forth. Freudian terminology and interpretation of behavior and motives permeates our society even today, when much of Freudian doctrine has been discredited or challenged and the world has changed sufficiently to make much of it inappropriate or inoperable. Nevertheless, human service delivery systems are structured as though all their clients lived in monogamous nuclear families, that is, they operate on a nine to five schedule that makes it very difficult for anyone to use their facilities except a housewife/mother. People who do not live in monogamous nuclear families are automatically labeled as deviant by these "helping" agencies, even though only a minority of the population fits their narrow definition of "normalcy." As long ago as 1972 50 per cent of the married females in the country worked outside the home, for starters. Over 16 million people headed single parent families. Five per cent of the population lived in extended families.

We pay through the nose for these services, which doubled in cost between 1968 and 1972 (*U.S. News & World Report*, 1972) and claimed that they are only for the poor, which is not true. Communication, criminal justice, economic, education, employment, health care, housing, political-legal, recreation, transportation, and welfare delivery systems affect the lives of every American. Our quality of life depends heavily on these human service delivery systems. Lack of control over such basic functions is not solely the problem of the poor.

A study of the practice of medicine in New York City by the then Public Health Commissioner during the 1960s revealed that the *same* physician often practiced a different brand of medicine in the teaching hospital, where students followed him around and the patients were largely publicly supported, in contrast to the private hospital, where he charged high prices. The appalling fact was that the public patients received the most excellent care and the private patients who paid the high fees got rather poor medical care!

As we indicated in the first chapter, the earmark of a real revolution in human affairs involves the reinterpretation of the facts of life in a manner that precludes the simultaneous acceptance of the old and new definitions. In the Freudian framework, for example, nonvaginal forms of sexual intercourse are labelled "deviant behavior." In the new "Pluralistic" interpretation (for want of a better name for a revolution that does not as yet have a name), if it feels good and doesn't harm anybody, it is acceptable behavior. In the old terms, childhood ended when the body matured and the child finished her/his education and became an adult. In the new terms, education is a lifelong involvement because we live in a world of change, not a stable world. The state of mind once associated with childhood, and lately identified with "youth" is a new stage inappropriately dreamed up by those who did not realize that a revolution was occurring. Openness to change and experience, trust, and willingness to adapt are the earmarks of the mature adult, who accepts the open-ended growth model of adulthood in place of the static closed model of the past.

The promise of democratic pluralism has been the hallmark of the "American Way" for hundreds of years, but up until now it has been only a promise. The reason our Constitution has been termed a "living document" is because the group of young men, most of them in their twenties and thirties, who wrote it did such an incredible job of stating the basics that they could be reinterpreted to apply to larger and larger groups of people over the years. Thus a document that once applied to males who were landowners and church members has been reinterpreted to include men who were unchurched and not landowners, men who were former slaves, and, finally, even women. Furthermore it was broadened to include single as well as married individuals. But over a space of 200 years, it has only recently been recognized that America's strength lies in its diversity—that we are not, in fact, the "great melting pot" that was part of the national self-image and goal for so many years. We are finally beginning to have the courage to recognize the value of difference, which was so carefully written into the Constitution but was largely ignored as a practical principle. In many areas of life, such as business, democratic pluralism was acknowledged and applauded, but in matters having to do with marriage, family life, and personal behavior, we remained bound by the point of view inherited from the Church courts which once ruled in such matters (Ramey, 1975b).

Today, privacy has finally become an issue; and the doctrine that "if it feels good and doesn't hurt anybody it is acceptable behavior" is part of the private behavior issue. It can be argued that this issue of democratic pluralism with respect to one's lifestyle couldn't become an issue until it became possible for the individual to sustain a household without a mate and even to raise children as a single individual if s/he so desires. The important thing is that the time is here—now.

In a pluralistic society the human service professional will deal with the client in terms of the client's lifestyle, not in terms of the client's deviation from the nuclear family lifestyle. This will change millions of diagnoses overnight, because millions of clients are labeled deviant simply because they do not live in a nuclear family (Ramey 1975c). This includes the Puerto Rican client who is living in a traditional extended family which is a part of his cultural heritage. A number of towns have passed "unrelated persons" ordinances specifically to keep Puerto Ricans out of their community. The Supreme Court ruled that it was legal to require that not more than two unrelated persons could live in a single-family dwelling. Some communities have used the desire to curtail college student living groups as a smoke screen for racial discrimination in the application of this ruling.

Which trends can we expect to continue and what new ones are developing as we enter the era of the pluralistic revolution? Here is a list of sixteen significant changes that will drastically alter the way we live.

1. Marriage is becoming a choice rather than an imperative; and it can be terminated by the female without leaving her stigmatized.

2. Marriage is becoming increasingly a peer relationship wherein the partners strive to achieve and maintain a morphogenic relationship rather than revert to the traditional "female as possession" pattern.

3. A growing trend toward nonmonogamy in both marriage and cohabitation.

4. A growing trend toward sexually open marriages in which intimate friendships are viewed as positively supportive of marriage and personal growth.

5. A continuing trend toward middle class cohabitation in place of marriage as a primary relationship pattern, especially on a temporary basis.

6. Rapid growth of deliberately childfree primary relationships.

7. An accelerating trend among women either to postpone marriage or to remain single, perhaps cohabiting from time to time. A similar but less pronounced trend may be expected among men.

8. A growing trend toward live-in situations involving couples and singles.

9. Significant erosion of the barriers between married and unmarried, and an increase in sexual intimacy across this barrier, especially between the unmarried and childfree or postchild couples.

10. Continued growth of the number of families in which all children are deliberately planned rather than occurring as "acts of God."

11. Continued acceleration of the divorce rate and slow down of the remarriage rate.

12. Further liberalization of law with respect to sexual activity among consenting adults.

13. Further relaxing of the promotion of monogamy by organized religion as the only acceptable form of marriage and an increase in the active exploration of alternatives to monogamy by organized religious groups.

14. Acceleration of the establishment of multi-adult households as a means of economic advantage and to replace kinship ties, with many of these groups growing out of intimate groups and networks.

15. Acceleration of the general trend toward fewer children in marriage, and formation of multi-adult households as a means of sharing fewer children among more adults. Some multi-adult households may be formed specifically for childbearing/rearing purposes.

16. Tacit recognition that various forms of complex living groups involve a number of positive aspects and gradual legal recognition of at least certain forms of complex living arrangements.

We believe these sixteen changes are among those going on right now that will have particular impact on the way we live and on the way we relate. As we consider the current concern for the population explosion, cultural variations in living, and the growing recognition of the distinction between loving and becoming a parent, we must not lose sight of the vast gulf between what we say and what we do. A careful study of actual birth control behavior among unmarried girls (Lindemann,

1975) indicates that sexually active young women, including teen-agers, go through three stages with respect to birth control. The first is the natural stage, during which they are not very active and are concerned about spontaneity and unpredictability. The second stage is the peer prescription stage in which they discuss birth control with friends and try out different methods. The third stage is the expert stage, when they actually seek out expert help with birth control. Even in this stage, Lindemann found that many young women do not see sex and pregnancy as a function of development. Instead, they associate both with marriage, with the result that even though sexually active, they have no concern with the implications of their sexual activity because they perceive marriage, not contraception, as the solution to the problem.

Thus it would seem that despite the fact that one out of four college students indicated that they planned to have no children, the reasonable expectation is that the majority of people will continue to get married and continue to have children, although they will probably have fewer children. The much heralded demise of the family is unlikely, despite the fact that it has some undesirable features, for in spite of those drawbacks the family has a lot going for it. What we do see coming is more people making a conscious choice to enter into marriage and less people being forced into it by their early socialization and by external pressures.

We do expect that the nature of being married will change, however. Already, several state legislatures are considering the legalization of trial marriage in some form. This step would effectively separate marriage for love only from marriage for becoming parents and would probably facilitate the continued shifting of marital interaction from the traditional male-dominant end of the spectrum toward the process-oriented peer relationship end. There will be a concurrent increase in transmarital intimacy.

Adultery is an integral part of monogamy, since neither can exist without the other; and with the advent of positive contraception it is likely that the incidence rate will continue to climb. Diffusion theory predicts that when a practice really catches on, the rate is likely to rise steeply in an "S" curve until it peaks out at near saturation level. Accordingly, we predict that adultery will come out of the closet much further than it already has, and that fidelity will be redefined as loyalty to one's primary relationship rather than as sexual exclusivity. It is not unreasonable to assume that as consensual transmarital intimacy increases, adultery will correspondingly fall into disfavor except among those who cling to the traditional marriage and corresponding need for secrecy about outside sexual relationships. In other words, when everybody is doing it, it will stop being clandestine for most people and they will once again interpret fidelity in terms of substance rather than form. But what about those who choose not to marry?

Cohabitation is often considered to include five forms. Two of those levels of the living-together relationship we have discussed separately as trial marriage and common law marriage. The other three are *casual arrangements,* which are usually nonexclusive relationships; exclusive but *temporary relationships,* where the couple have no definite plans for the future; and *stable relationships,* in which the couple assumes their relationship to be secure, enduring, and likely to last for a while (Danziger and Greenwall, 1973). Most people, when asked, say that they have a stable relationship, even though they neither have plans for future marriage nor expect to live together permanently. The percentage of individuals choosing intermittent cohabitation as a nonmarital relating pattern, especially in the 25–55 age group, is increasing many times faster than the percentage getting married.

People who are cohabiting almost unanimously consider cohabitation a realistic alternative to marriage as long as there are no children. It is already legal in twelve states, which have passed "Consenting Adults" statutes (California, Colorado, Connecticut, Delaware, Hawaii, Illinois, Maine, New Mexico, North Dakota, Ohio, Oregon, and Washington) to cohabit. The extension of such recognition to other states may well become the de facto route to reserving marriage for becoming a parent.

There appears to be a marked growth in the number of live-in situations involving married couples and a single male or female. Interest in this practice is also spreading. Some individuals who have tried swinging soon graduated to an interest in a semi-permanent three-cornered relationship. A three-person relationship, as we have indicated before, is probably the easiest complex relationship to manage, once you have surmounted the difficulties of a two person relationship. For the single person, there are two predominant reasons given for entering into such an arrangement. The first, usually put forward by someone who has not been married, is that they regard the trio as a transition step which is closer to being in a primary relationship than casual dating or casual cohabitation because the other two partners already have a stable, enduring relationship. These individuals see advantages in becoming part of such a household because it gives them better insight into the pros and cons of getting into a primary relationship themselves.

The second reason comes from previously married individuals, some of whom have children to raise, and focuses on the desire to be part of an adult marriage without getting married. Such persons may not be able to get married or may feel so put off by the indignities of the courtship "rat race" that they refuse to participate in it. It is not uncommon to find the single person with this point of view in the 45–70 age bracket. The older the single people, the more likely they are to feel compelling reasons for not getting married, such as the loss of Social Security benefits, if female, or the opposition of children to a parent getting married because of the potential loss of their inheritance.

The couple who adds a single to its household may offer a variety of reasons, ranging from interest in three-way intimacy to relief of some of the pressure of raising children in a two-person household. Often the third person is taken in temporarily to carry him/her over a crisis of some sort and all three discover that they like living together well enough to continue doing so. A widower physician in his late fifties welcomed his niece and her husband into his home when the husband first returned from service in Vietnam. The three got along so well that it soon became apparent that they would all rather stay together than not, especially after the two men discovered that they were bisexuals. In another instance, two couples had been intimate friends for some time when one husband divorced his wife and left the city. His wife moved in with the other couple and, two years later, she is still there.

Singles are a much greater threat to a child-centered couple than to a childfree couple. It is therefore not surprising that there is a growing amount of sexual intimacy across the boundary between singles and childfree couples; but there is very little activity of this sort between singles and child-centered couples, except where the single is also child-centered.

The Church has begun to modify its stand against non-monogamy. The Unitarians, Quakers, and Presbyterians in particular appear to be questioning old beliefs and encouraging experimentation with various marriage alternatives. The Lutherans and Northern Baptists have also sponsored workshops for the exploration of human sexuality and marriage alternatives.

It is still too early to see clearly the impact of the pill, the IUD, and sterilization on birth control. As we have stated elsewhere, 30 percent of the population that practices birth control has chosen the pill, the IUD, or permanent sterilization in order to have complete freedom from worries about contraception. Still, there are a lot of people not practicing birth control, especially among teenagers. Over fifty per cent of the 401,000 illegitimate babies born in 1971 were to teenagers.

It is hard to believe that all of these children were wanted. Add the children born to parents who already have the number they wanted to have, but who have suffered contraceptive "slip up" of some sort, and it becomes apparent that in spite of the availability of positive contraception, a lot more children are being born than are desired. We can therefore foresee a continued decline of the overall birth rate and a concurrent very positive trend toward all children being wanted and planned for. It is encouraging to note that between 1970 and 1973 the illegitimacy rate declined 12 per cent for white teenagers and a whopping 23 per cent for black teenagers. Already there are some people setting up complex living groups in order to provide ideal living arrangements for childrearing, according to their interpretation of what is ideal for this purpose. In most instances they cite as ideals more adult–child interaction, multiple models for the children, better life-support, and greater concern for the growth environment. There is no conclusive evidence that children will only thrive in a certain type of environment, however. In fact most evidence with respect to childrearing deals only with the negative—what kind of environment will stunt growth—and even that data is inconclusive.

Ellie is 28. Her son David is now ten. He was conceived three weeks before Ellie's 18th birthday. She was waiting until she was 18 to get the pill because at 18 she could do so without her mother knowing about it; but three weeks before the magic date her boyfriend talked her into intercourse. To her everlasting chagrin, that one time was enough to make her pregnant. She decided to have the baby and marry her boyfriend even though he was a year younger than she and still in high school. The marriage lasted two and a half years, during which time she provided 80 per cent of the support for the new family. She finally got rid of her irresponsible husband, who had previously gotten another girl pregnant, and he went home to mother, who paid his tuition so he could go to college.

Ellie found a job, found a daytime sitter for David, and went to work full time. After six or eight months, she also enrolled in college, and somehow managed to go to college full time while supporting herself and David. She completed her B.A. and continued her work as a real estate agent. Soon she had a broker's license and, as a side line, was buying and refurbishing houses and then selling them. Today she is a successful businesswoman who takes a dim view of remarriage. "I'm still waiting for a man to come along that I can get to accept me as I am," she says. David has developed into a highly social little boy and has made rapid strides in school. He seems well adjusted, self reliant, and has learned to cook, clean house, and shop as well as to read the maps and look for the clues when he goes Corvette Club road racing with his mother.

Ellie's sexually open philosophy of life soon led her into an intimate group of friends that have largely sufficed to meet her intimacy needs without establishing a new primary relationship, although she still expects that she will establish such a relationship in the future. Her friend Jody has also combined career and children very effectively. Jody is manager and part owner of a restaurant. Her husband Tony is a marine biologist. They have two children, Tony Jr. and Stella, ages ten and seven. Jody works from noon until midnight three days a week and her partner, Steve, works the same hours the other three days of the week. Tony arranged his courses at the University so that he is free during the afternoons and evenings of the days Jody works. When there are scheduling problems, he takes the responsibility for arranging a sitter.

Jody and Tony have a peer primary relationship. Because of the nature of his job, Tony was able to share in the childrearing tasks to a much greater extent than some men, although as he likes to point out, executives have great "physical presence" latitude in their jobs and most of them could take off for home emergencies if they really wanted to. Tony also feels that children should be exposed to their parents' career worlds if at all possible. He therefore takes one or the other of the children with him on field trips from time to time, and he has taken each of them to several out of town conferences. Jody has followed the same practice, introducing the children to wholesalers, showing them how the restaurant operates, and instructing them about how to plan in a business operation.

All three children in these two examples are aware of the difference in their parents' lifestyle as compared to that of other kids' parents. They measure the difference in terms of the warm friendly atmosphere of many involved adults whom their parents love and who love their parents. They view this as a fortunate difference between their homes and their friends' homes. They feel included in the relatively open loving atmosphere because many family activities involve intimate friends of their parents and the children of those friends. Lately Tony, Jody, and Ellie have been taking a hard look at the pros and cons of buying a house together and forming a complex living group.

It would not be surprising if Tony, Jody, and Ellie do get together in a complex living group. Many such groups form out of intimate friendships; and they tend to be more successful than those groups that come together through advertising or a notice on a bulletin board. As more of these groups allow themselves to become visible as responsible, respectable, nonthreatening community members, more and more lower-middle and working class people can be expected to be attracted to the considerable economic and childrearing advantages of complex living groups. Most families find that by living in a complex living group of working individuals they can cut down on their expenses. In one group in the middle west, composed of three couples and their children, a sixty per cent reduction in expenses was achieved even though only the three adult males were employed. This is a substantial saving indeed. Yet in spite of these positive aspects of complex living groups, we do not believe that they will become a major factor in American life. It is estimated that there are now fewer than a million people living in complex groups. Even if this number triples it would still amount to less than 1.5 per cent of the population.

11

The Growing Importance
of Intimate Groups and Networks

During her senior year Cynthia went to the American Physics Association annual meeting where she met Larry, a graduate student at LSU. He was so enthusiastic about LSU that she sent an application to their graduate program as well as to the University of Texas and to Texas A&M. Just before graduation Larry called her and invited her to come to an end-of-the-year departmental party at LSU. She enjoyed herself at the party and was impressed with the people on the staff, but most of all, she really enjoyed spending the whole weekend with Larry. When she was accepted at both Texas and LSU she quickly decided in favor of LSU.

Once on campus, Cynthia was surprised that the first person Larry introduced her to was Doris, explaining that they had lived together when both were juniors and that Doris now lived with his good friend, Bo. It was obvious that Larry and Doris were still close, and Cynthia was not prepared to find Doris so friendly when Larry introduced Cynthia as the girl he had had the great weekend with after the departmental party. This did not seem to be a problem for Doris, although Cynthia could have cheerfully cut his tongue out for saying it.

Within a few short weeks, Cynthia discovered a whole new world—the world of intimate friendship. She had never before met a man who was completely open about his other intimate relationships, nor had she met people who introduced their lovers to each other. Yet she found considerable relief in the openness of this group of people who either had gone to bed together, were now lovers, or expected that they might some day go to bed with each other. She found a place to live right across the street from Bo and Doris and found that Adrian, another member of the group, also lived there. Soon she and Adrian became fast friends, and before long she realized that the year was almost over and that she had not been lonely or depressed about being transplanted into another state, as she had expected to be. In her circle, these friends were so supportive of each other that she hadn't had much time for being lonely. She found that somehow the fact that sexual intimacy was permissible and taken for granted in their group made the relationships more important to her because much of the courting, preening, and intrigue were eliminated. When Bo went to bed with her, Doris was happy for them both, and she spent the night with Adrian. Just before the end of the semester Cynthia finally got together with Roger, another member of the group, during an all night jam session on Bourbon Street in New Orleans. Soon she was seeing Roger exclusively; and after graduation, during which each picked up their M.A. diplomas, Cynthia and Roger got married.

Intimate groups and networks have existed throughout history, no doubt, but only recently has there been much recognition of their existence. With the new openness about sex, it has become easier for researchers to locate respondents willing to talk about such groups, and it has also become permissible to write about them. It may come as a shock to many people to learn that such networks include grandparents and even great-grandparents, for sexually open or peer marriage is decidedly not a new invention. One study has located individuals who have practiced open or peer marriage for over twenty years—long before the current interest in this practice surfaced in the press (Ramey, 1975a).

One of the positive features of intimate friendship is its ability to provide a bridge, as it did for Cynthia, between leaving home and setting up a primary relationship. For others it suffices so adequately for closeness, companionship, and sexual intimacy that a primary relationship is indefinitely, sometimes permanently, postponed. This appears to be true both of young never-married individuals and older previously married individuals. Intimate groups and networks form among the very young as well as among the elderly, although most seem to involve a wide age range with many participants in their thirties, forties and fifties. Over the next 15 years this age range will become more and more heavily weighted at the younger end. One group, in which the average age today is 20.5, began with several people who met in elementary school. Sexual intimacy began for some participants in eighth grade. The group of 31 includes two married couples, one couple that has cohabited and one couple currently cohabiting. This is the youngest intimate group we have ever heard about, and it already has a seven year history. It is particularly noteworthy because unlike the other groups we know about, this one involves predominantly lower-middle and working class individuals. However, 60 per cent of the members are in college or have graduated. The age range in this group today is from 18 to 29, and both the youngest and the oldest are women.

The importance of studying younger groups lies in the issue of whether or not they continue to carry over into later life their practical elimination of the barrier between married and single, the predominance of singles in the group, and the number who continue to cohabit rather than marry long after they finish college. In one network with an average age of 32, 50 per cent of the members are single, including three who are divorced, while in the aforementioned study of 380 individuals, two out of three were married. In this latter study the average age was 44 for the males and 41 for the females, but the range was from sixteen to sixty-four.

The development of intimate friendships through the practice of sexually open marriage or peer marriage as well as on the part of single individuals appears to represent a shift in attitudes about sexual intimacy and the ability of monogamous marriage to meet the need for intimacy, stability, companionship, and the need for continued personal growth. Until we conduct a random sample study of upper-middle class individuals however, we will not be able to say with any degree of certainty that this is not simply a previously unreported upper-middle class practice. There is a notorious dearth of reports on friendship patterns among the upper-middle class, so we simply do not know how unusual or usual intimate groups and networks are. Russell Lynes wrote a book in 1953 called a *Surfeit of Honey* in which he described the "upper bohemians" in terms that provide almost an exact fit with the description of the previously mentioned sample of 380 respondents, except for one item. He did not say a single word about sexual intimacy. Perhaps he knew that in 1953 his book might not have been published if he had mentioned sex. A proposal to replicate the first study of intimate groups and networks using a randomized upper-middle class population sample is now being written in the hope of clarifying this important issue. In 1970 Stoller wrote an article about intimate networks in which he emphasized the potential values for families in sharing intimately. He completely ignored the possibility that there might be sexual intimacy or that intimate sharing might lead to sexual sharing, however. He also concerned himself solely with nuclear families. Otto (1971) carried on this theme after Stoller's death, but he also failed to deal with sexual sharing as a possible concomitant of intimate clusters of people. It was Larry and Joan Constantine, who, in 1970, first suggested that intimate networks would logically involve sexual as well as non-sexual intimacy.

If one partner in a peer-bond develops an intimate friendship with a third person, the other member of the peer-bond is also likely to become friendly with that person sooner or later, and perhaps with that person's mate as well, if there is one. As chains of intimate relationships grow, a group of like-minded individuals becomes identified, and subsequent intimate friendships are likely to be formed from among this group. In this way, those interested in forming deeply meaningful friendships short circuit the lengthy process of discovering whether or not someone is on the same wavelength by developing contacts from within a known universe of people with the same philosophy of life. The kind of group or network that slowly emerges from these choices is heavy on the relationship side and rather light on the sexual intimacy side. In the sample of 380 people, 68 per cent were "associated members"—individuals who were intimate sexually with at least one person in the group other than his/her mate; assuming he/she had a mate. Twenty-four per cent were core members—identified as those each of whom had been sexually intimate at least heterosexually with several other core members. The remaining 8 per cent (affiliated members) had not been intimate sexually with anyone in the group other than a mate, assuming there was one. Since membership depends upon philosophy of life rather than upon sexual contact, that is, all of the people in the group or network identify "Joe" as a member, some individuals have been in intimate friendship groups for fifteen years and have not actualized the potential for sexual intimacy within the group. Some groups have no core members at all.

Individuals report that they became involved in intimate friendships because of sexual attraction or a desire for deeper sharing with friends (through which one can have deeper sharing with one's own partner, if in a primary relationship). Also, the availability of sexual sharing among friends reduces the need to court or test (thus reducing the amount of actual sexual intimacy in the light of open acceptance of potential intimacy), which greatly enhances friendship. Finally, individuals become involved through exposure to new ideas in books, plays, movies, and the media.

According to its practitioners, as we have previously indicated, intimate friendship is built on the philosophy of open acceptance of *potential* sexual intimacy rather than on sexual involvement, per se. One reason sexual intimacy is seen as an important vector in intimate friendship, along with social, intellectual, emotional, family, and career intimacy, is that the vulnerability associated with making love serves as a shortcut method of establishing extremely candid grounds for relating that might take months or years to build in nonsexual relating. Everybody in the nation moves every five years on the average, but people in the upper-middle class career groups represented in this study are likely to move as often as every two or three years. These people have a sense of time breathing down their necks. They have also, for the most part, left kinship and family ties far behind them. For these reasons they are especially interested in establishing friendship support systems quickly. In the normal course of events, it could take two years to develop a friendship about to the point where, with luck, it would be sufficiently deep and open to provide support for an individual or couple without any other ties in the community. But in two years' time they could well be about to move again. If instead they join an intimate group or network, one to which they may well have been introduced before arriving in town because of intercity links to a previously known group, they can expect to develop close personal ties very quickly. Over time, networks spread further and further; and in some cases they even become international, so that it becomes possible to travel extensively and still stay within the intimate friendship network.

In the sample of 380 intimate friendship participants mentioned earlier, 87 per cent of the men ranked career first among life satisfactions, while 95 per cent of the women ranked family or love relationships first. The ranking was reversed for the second most important life satisfaction: 67 per cent of the men ranked family or love relationships second and 82 per cent of the women ranked career or occupation second. Intimate friendships held the third highest ranking for the women, at 78 per cent, but were ranked fourth by the men at 46 per cent, one percentage point behind community or political involvement. Nonintimate friendships ranked sixth with the men, at 22 per cent, and fifth with the women, at 34 per cent.

This large gap between intimate friends and other friends fits with the comments of respondents that their nonintimate friends seem so uninvolved and superficial that they have systematically weeded them out, because there just isn't enough time for superficial relationships. Many respondents had not previously identified their intimate friendships as being any different from their other friendships until after discussing them in a seminar, workshop, or personal conversation dealing with this topic. Singles, in particular, seemed to feel that their relationships were somehow different from those of married couples, and that they could not be intimate friendships because they were part of the normal dating behavior among pre-marrieds. Not until we defined and discussed intimate friendship as a way of relating openly and honestly that acknowledged the sexual aspect of living to be no more or less important than any other aspect of life, so that it was appropriate to consider sexual intimacy in any relationship between friends, did they grasp the significant difference between friendship in general and intimate friendship. As one bachelor put it, "You're talking about the difference between friends who acknowledge the possibility of sexual intimacy between them and accept the appropriateness of such sexual intimacy even though they may not immediately act on this understanding, and those who pretend such a possibility does not exist or refuse to discuss it or really aren't interested, period."

Kelly and Stephanie have been intimate friends for many years, ever since they met in the maternity ward where each was involved in the wonder of a first-born child. There they discovered that they lived only a half-mile apart and that their husbands, Art and Leslie, both worked in the local government. The two couples became friends as they shared information and problems concerning their growing children and babysat for each other. Kelly and Stephanie spent a lot of time together and were quite open with one another about the sensual overtones of nursing and baby care that they discovered both felt. Kelly was a science fiction fan, and early in 1962 she read Heinlein's new book, *Stranger in a Strange Land* and discussed its interesting view of intimacy with Stephanie. In exploring the bisexual theme in the story, the two were able to admit to sexual feelings for each other, and after several weeks of talking it through, their relationship became sexually intimate. Each was afraid to discuss the new relationship with her husband, however, and their relationship remained a secret for several years.

In 1964 Art brought his assistant, Emily, home to dinner one night, and after dinner he initiated a conversation that lasted until three the next morning. What he had to say surprised both Kelly and Emily, for he announced that he was very attracted to Emily and wanted to go to bed with her but he felt that, in fairness to both of them, he could not broach the subject to her or to Kelly without the other being present. He made it very clear that his desire had nothing to do with loving Kelly less or with wanting to change their relationship in any way, and that he was not looking to establish a new or secondary primary relationship but simply was hoping that Emily might share his desire to deepen their existing relationship by adding a sexual dimension to it.

Kelly was completely overwhelmed with remorse about her secret affair with Stephanie in the face of Art's straightforward approach to the possibility of a sexual relationship outside their marriage. Art and Emily both misinterpreted her sudden pallor and wild tears. As quickly as she could, she reassured them and asked Art to call Stephanie and ask her to come over right away. Without understanding why, Art did as she requested, and in less than five minutes Stephanie arrived. In control of herself by this time, Kelly told Stephanie what was going on and explained that under the circumstances she had to clear the air before she could let Art proceed any further, but felt that she could not do so without Stephanie in the conversation.

Art and Kelly agreed to open their marriage as a result of that long night; and Kelly didn't feel like such a heel after Art admitted that he had had an affair lasting several months himself earlier in their marriage, and that it was his feeling of guilt about that relationship that had prompted him to take a different approach to outside sexual intimacy this time. Emily, as it turned out, already knew several people who were intimate friends, and she volunteered to introduce Kelly, Art, and Stephanie to them so that they could discuss the problems, responsibilities, and joys of open relating with people who were knowledgeable about it.

Almost fifteen years later, there are over twenty people in this network, including Stephanie's husband Leslie, who accepts the philosophy of open relating but has not to this day actualized the potential. He is quite involved with the participants in their group in other ways however, particularly in the family and community interest aspects of relating. The members of this network agree with the list of disadvantages usually cited by those practicing sexually open relating. The biggest problem is lack of time.

Just managing to find time for deeply committed relationships outside the primary relationship is extremely difficult for busy people. For those not in a primary relationship, this problem is often expressed in terms of multiple relationships, none of which are quite primary, and the feeling of being torn between them but not wanting to make any one primary. Scheduling difficulties seem to be especially troublesome for those who have children, but on the other hand, such difficulties serve to redistribute roles between husband and wife in such a way as to make the demands of parenthood much more of a shared responsibility than is usually the case. Some husbands admit that although they may have talked about sharing for many years, they never really understood what sharing meant until their wives began making outside plans that necessitated their managing on their own with the kids. One husband who had agreed with his wife many years before that each was free to have outside sexual relationships actualized this agreement several times before his wife acted upon it the first time. When she finally did, he found himself totally involved in four days of domestic chores that he had never been completely responsible for in eight years of marriage. His appreciation of his wife grew by leaps and bounds as he struggled with the needs of three children, a dog, and two rabbits while his wife flew to the Bahamas.

Babysitting ranks third among the problems or disadvantages, closely followed by sleeping arrangements. Sleeping over is very important to many intimate friends but it may raise serious problems for them, especially if the arrangement could result in someone being present but left out. Nobody wants to be left out, and consequently, few people are likely to leave someone else out.

Another drawback is the problem of interruptions. The fear of being interrupted is in itself enough to put a damper on many people; and this is especially a problem for people with roommates and those with children. Single parents are perhaps in a worse bind than anyone else with respect to scheduling, babysitting, sleeping arrangements, and interruptions.

One further difficulty often mentioned is "situational complexity." Situations often arise that interfere with one's ability to relate intimately. In the group mentioned earlier, Emily's mother came to Seattle and stayed with her for six weeks after Emily's father died, which made things very complex indeed.

In the intimate groups and networks study, participants said that 72 per cent of the time they spent together was devoted to social activity. Such activity ranged from attending parties, lectures, plays, and concerts to simply getting together to talk. About half of these encounters involved petting, cuddling, or touching to some degree; and nearly the same amount of time was spent in discussion and problem-solving situations. One third of the time was recreational in nature, including participatory and nonparticipatory sports, as well as noncompetitive recreational activities and games or other forms of shared relaxation. Business activities were a part of one quarter of the time spent with intimate friends, and sexual intimacy was involved in 19 per cent of their time together. Hobbies were involved 16 per cent of the time, family 13 per cent of the time, travel 12 per cent of the time, and community or political activities 6 per cent of the time. Obviously several different activities occurred simultaneously much of the time.

Respondents often report that sex is unimportant in their relationships, relatively speaking, but that they couldn't have had such deep and meaningful friendships without the potential sexual intimacy. Freedom to talk about very personal matters with friends of *both* sexes, not just those of one's own sex, and to have the benefit of both married and single points of view on personal problems, is highly valued. For the unmarried, especially, intimate friendship provides a bridge to the "married mainstream" of American life without forcing them into marriage in order to enjoy it.

Intimate friends become quite involved in each other's lives. In several instances we found them going into business together. Older established participants may help their younger friends get established in their careers by recommending them to clients, bringing them in on deals, lending them money, or pushing their careers in other ways. Some are jointly active in community affairs or in the political arena. Others share hobbies or travel together. But the major involvement is in joint social and problem-solving activity. This tendency of intimate friendship to add supportive social and economic ties between participants of different generations also serves to develop longer geographic ties in some instances, so that participants are more likely to resist outside (career) pressures to move geographically in order to move up the career ladder. As a matter of fact, this can also be a contributing factor to breaking up an intimate friendship.

Intimate friendships terminate because of growing apart in general interests, unequal attraction, one or the other person moving away, one person feeling left behind in terms of growth, too much social pressure, deterioration of a primary relationship, and growing too close for the comfort of some intimate friends. This last reason, as mentioned above, can result from a group coming closer—in fact considering entering into a group living arrangement—which may be too much proximity for some participants. There are those who favor intimate friendship precisely because it offers the opportunity to be close without the obligation to be close all the time, since the participants do not live together. The older the individual, the less likely s/he is to be willing to give up this freedom to withdraw temporarily by entering into a group living situation. The other reasons cited for leaving an intimate friendship are essentially the same as for ending any other friendship.

As the number of open marriages, and particularly peer relationships, grows, so will the intimate groups and networks in which singles as well as couples are full participants, in which homosexual and bisexual relationships cross over freely with heterosexual relationships, and in which racial barriers cease to exist. Most of those who were involved in intimate groups and networks in the past were upper-middle class individuals who had strong convictions about what was right for them regardless of the opinions of others. Now that their ground-breaking individualistic stance has become the rallying point of an entire generation, we can expect a rapid shift in the average age of participants as young people swell the ranks of those who believe "what is good for us and harms no one else is right."

There is no way of guessing how many people are in intimate groups and networks today, but the number is probably already significant (Mazur, 1973). After trial marriage, intimate friendship will probably be the most widely practiced alternate lifestyle in the years to come. This statement assumes that "trial marriage" will be the polite fiction term applied to cohabitation which is not intended to involve childbearing/rearing, or that a legally defined and accepted trial or nonchildbearing marriage form will be adopted that is distinct from "parenting marriage." If such a legal form were adopted, and it did not involve sexual exclusivity, then adultery would become far less prevalent, because adultery can only exist in a monogamous or sexually exclusive marriage framework.

If people were able to be open and accepting about outside relationships, then intimate friendship would indeed become widespread. A more conservative and realistic short term prediction is that most people of all ages will continue to get married and to live in what purport to be sexually exclusive monogamous relationships, and that a majority of these individuals will practice adultery on the side. How soon this state of affairs will change is hard to predict. As we have said before, the best research information to date suggests that young people who cohabit in college get married (usually not to each other) and settle down into rather conventional traditional marriages soon after leaving college. Unless this general trend changes, or we learn that these marriages soon metamorphize into open or peer marriages or break up because they cannot do so, we will not really know which way things are going. However, the Constantines (1975) say that the age 20–25 married group today has already experienced more transmarital sexual intimacy than all other age groups have experienced in their entire married lives.

Although changes are occurring all along the age curve in American life, it may be that massive change must occur at the earlier age level first and then spread forward into later years.

The premarital sexual revolution has already taken place, completely and unequivocally. It has occurred in two steps: first, in terms of premarital sexual experience (Udry, 1974) and now in terms of premarital cohabitation experience (Macklin, 1974). The next major change appears to be occurring in the first marriage pattern among people in their twenties, where we find four significant trends: a trend toward shorter first marriages, particularly among those in their early twenties, a trend toward more and earlier transmarital sexual experience (L & J Constantine 1975), a trend toward putting off marriage, and a trend toward later first pregnancy and fewer children (Perrucci and Targ, 1974).

If the growing impact of the pluralistic revolution continues at the pace of the premarital intercourse and cohabitation shifts, then the marital shift in the twenties age range should take about ten years or so to become normative practice. With the population bulge now developing among people in this age group, the average age of the population is getting younger. We can, therefore, expect that an overall shift from a Freudian to a pluralistic image of society may possibly occur within the next ten to fifteen years. The measure of general acceptance of intimate friendships will provide a ready index to the degree of transition to democratic pluralism in lifestyle choices.

12

Multiadult Households of the Future: What Can We Expect?

It is an ironic paradox that the pursuit of independence—our fierce struggle to be self-actualized, self-contained, self-sufficient individuals—leads us pell-mell into the interdependent world of the pluralistic revolution. Humans grow through their relationships. The problem-solving urge does not take kindly to working in a vacuum. Stripping down society to its single indivisible unit, the individual, and presenting that individual with the biological and technological capability of survival alone in a viable but singular household, turns out to be selling humanity's birthright for a mess of pottage. The man or woman who chooses the celibate existence, abjuring relationships with others, whether of a social, sexual, intellectual, or emotional nature, soon finds him or herself cut off from the problems that define life itself. A life without problems to solve isn't worth living. One soon becomes overwhelmingly bored with it all because a life without problems is a life without growth.

The partial withdrawal from life practiced in the monasteries of yesteryear, replete with vows of silence and chastity, involved much common activity and a firm and all-pervading sense of community. And yet even in that atmosphere of community, the problem of physical and mental aberration was omnipresent and directly related to the degree of isolation practiced. We need problem-solving interaction with others. For many people, dyadic marriage meets this need, for others it is not enough.

The difficulty with dyadic marriage is less that it puts down the individual than that it cannot suffice to open up the individual. Mary loves to play bridge, but Jerry dislikes card games. Mary and Jerry get married. Mary gives up bridge. Jerry, on the other hand, gives up camping because Mary is not interested in outdoor things. If you are married, stop and think for a minute of the things you either gave up, modified, or failed to pursue because the couple-front demanded of the married couple did not allow you to do otherwise. While you are at it, think about the people you gave up—and the ones who give you up. We do not invite people unless we find both husband and wife acceptable to both of us. That means that we do not see many people that we *both* like, let alone those that only one of us likes, because we do not both like their mates.

Enlarging the circle changes the situation drastically. In a three- or more person group each has many more opportunities to find mutually acceptable interests. In Chapter Two we said the individual could make any one of three choices about relating to others. S/he could choose to avoid all relationships, s/he could choose only relationships that did not involve a primary commitment, or s/he could choose a primary commitment. We pointed out that this third choice might nominally exclude other relationships, although in all likelihood, even in a so-called monogamous relationship, the odds are against exclusivity. It could also include a variety of other possible relationships.

It has been argued by some that the very complexity of complex living groups, group marriage, and the like will prevent most people from ever undertaking to live in such settings. We humans have lived in many different cultural and social settings, including very complex living arrangements, for millennia. The problem is not one of capability at all, but rather one of desirability. In a society that has pushed the notion of independence for centuries, it is easy to confuse the issue by pitting

autonomy against commitment and deciding that autonomy is equivalent to growth and commitment equal to stagnation. Dogmatic acceptance of this equation without asking the key question, "Commitment to what?" can leave one looking pretty silly, for it is in *groups* committed to growth that the most noticeable growth occurs, not in individuals committed to autonomy.

Intimate groups and networks provide a transitional step between living alone and the dyadic primary relationship, as well as between the dyadic primary relationship and multiple primary relationships. Intimate friendships within the group exhibit the same wide range of commitment and complexity, from very loose to extremely interactive ties, that is masked by the stereotypical dyadic relationship. This allows the individual to adjust his/her relationships to the ebb and flow of his/her needs, desires, and time, not to mention his/her ability to cope at the moment. As we discussed earlier, the various links may provide any or several of the kinds of interaction a person needs or enjoys, ranging from support to instruction to nurturing, and from social to intellectual challenge. Mary may play bridge with Betty, provide intellectual stimulation to Joe, and help Estelle set up a blood bank, while Jerry is giving emotional support to Pete, writing with Nancy, and scuba-diving with both.

Because our society is so insistent on the values of individualism, it is difficult to predict how soon a significant change may occur in the direction of realizing that more growth will take place in an enriched environment than in a restricted one. That the change is happening, there can be little doubt. As Phil Slater (1974) pointed out, the media and advertising quickly pick up newly voiced truths and claim them for their own; and even if the claim is a lie, the fact that they attempt to climb onto the bandwagon lends verification to the underlying truth. Public disbelief of their claims forces businesses to modify their behavior in an attempt to prove that their claims are justified. We see evidence all around us that individualism is being redefined to include growth, if it is to be accepted as *positive* rather than negative individualism. Slowly but inevitably this modification

must lead to pluralism in lifestyles. It is sometimes easier to see where an issue is going when you ask the question: "What negatives are being voiced against the direction of travel?" In the case of personal growth and freedom, the answer comes back loud and clear in the warnings against losing one's self in multiple relationships and especially in multiple adult households where "there is no privacy!"

Privacy is, of course, essential now and then in order to think through what is happening; but we make it a fetish in our society. Many housewives would love to have a great deal *less* privacy, for they are stuck with great gobs of it when their kids are in school; and if they have no children, the situation often is worse yet. Their husbands, who have been away at the office interacting with others all day, may well come home hoping to find some privacy, only to be met by a mate starving for adult companionship. In a multi- adult household neither would have such a severe problem. There would be other adults for the wife to interact with, probably during the day as well as in the evening, so that she would have less need to monopolize her husband's time in the evening. This would afford him the opportunity to spend some time alone if he wished, too.

What forms are multi- adult households likely to take in the future, given the changes that must occur in society's attitudes with respect to privacy and growth? If current trends continue, we can expect to see the greatest growth in households of eight or fewer adults, particularly trios and tetrads (mostly two couple tetrads). Trios and tetrads are the most common form of multi- adult household today because they fit so easily into the existing social order and are the easiest to put together and sustain. There are so many acceptable reasons for three or four people to be living together that the general public seldom questions them. A third person might be a boarder, a ward, a relative, a friend, an employee, a business associate, or simply a visitor. Two couple situations are easily explained as "sharing a house." Many groups don't bother to explain at all, and find that nobody asks for an explanation.

As the number of people in intimate groups and networks

increases, so will the number in multi- adult households of eight or less spawned by intimate groups and networks. Larger commune-type complex living groups do not usually come from intimate groups, however. They generally develop out of religious and/or utopian or drop-out philosophies or they arise from the economic needs of students while in college. Generally speaking, they occur at an earlier stage in life, whereas the kind of groups that spring from intimate groups or networks generally develop in the thirties and beyond. So far, only a few people in intimate groups and networks appear to "escalate" into complex living groups. We do not know whether there is any particular trend with respect to this practice; but if the ratio remains constant and the number of individuals in intimate groups and networks increases dramatically, as we suspect may happen, then the number in complex living groups of eight or less adults would likewise increase.

We have devoted our attention to non-drop-out multi- adult households in this book because we feel that they will have much greater significance in the future than the religious or utopian communes. The liklihood of a significant increase in the number of utopian or religious communes or complex living groups is slim because membership in such groups requires a radical departure from the mainstream culture. Small groups of the type we have described in Chapter Nine, on the other hand, are in the mainstream tradition of banding together to accomplish mutual aims within the social structure. They involve several outcomes that are highly regarded in the United States, including en- hanced economic status and better child nurturing, not to mention a greater degree of personal freedom because of the economic and numerical enhancement of the family unit. Our complex living group research has focused exclusively on such groups and many of the observations in this chapter are based on that research.

It is relatively easy to start a multi- adult group quietly by adding a third party or another couple to an existing couple. We have already mentioned the dramatic increase in the number of people looking for a couple or a single to create a live-in temporary threesome. Although most of these arrangements are indeed temporary, some survive; and especially noteworthy is the fact that ex-participants often look for a different combination, and may, after several false starts, find a trio that fits well enough to consider an indefinite arrangement.

These multi- adult households of eight or less will in the future fall both within the trial marriage framework and the parenting marriage framework, assuming the society legitimizes these two forms of marriage. In such an event, these complex living groups will qualify as group marriages if the participants each have multi-primary relationships in the group. If the definition of marriage not only is divided into trial marriage and parenting marriage, but also is enlarged to include more than two adult members, as it may be, then all such groups would automatically become group marriages whether they involved double primary relationships for each participant or not. This is an important distinction, because the legal presumption today does not agree with the behavioral reality today, that is, the law presumes a primary relationship in marriage that often does not exist in fact. Thus the standard that I apply to group marriage, and with which the Constantines' (1973) agree, is a much stricter definition of marriage than the legal one for dyadic marriage.

Without the blanket legal definition, most of these groups will not be defined as group marriages in the sense of each person having dual primary relationships, but will instead be live-in situations or complex living groups. In practical terms there may be little difference in the two types of household; but in terms of self-image and degree of commitment to the relationship, the two are worlds apart. Group marriage is the most complex form of multiple commitment we can conceive; and as such it involves an overwhelming amount of investment of time and psyche, and entails much more responsibility and willingness to work through problems. For these reasons, I have little expectation of a great increase in the number of group marriages. The Constantines' (1973) estimate that there are perhaps as many as a thousand group marriages in America today. If this number increases to

10,000 in the next ten years, I will be amazed; and if it should increase to 50,000, I would be astounded.

We have already discussed the economic advantages of complex living groups at some length. We have not talked about the issue that more people ask questions about than any other—namely, sex. The major underlying reason for the growth of multiperson households is the opportunity they provide for shared intimacy, including sexual intimacy; but the sexual ground rules vary wildly from group to group and within the same group over time. Some groups are celibate, at least for some period of time. Others practice free love and make strong efforts to break up couples by requiring them to have separate rooms and by requesting that they not spend more time with each other than with other members of the group. Some groups are strictly monogamous on a couple basis, and it is unusual for a single to survive in such a group because the couple-front is often inpenetrable. Some groups involve sexually open marriages, although not necessarily peer marriages. Some groups involve group marriage. Any of the relational formats may be heterosexual, homosexual, or bisexual, but monogamous groups rarely include any but heterosexual relationships. Interracial groups are rare, but almost all groups are either irreligious or interreligious. Sexually open groups that developed out of intimate groups or networks are the most likely to be bisexual and/or multiracial. Groups with a mixed sexual mode, for example, some that are monogamous and others that are sexually open, have a low survival probability. In one group that involved three monogamous couples, the group broke up after one woman read *Proposition 31* and wanted the group to discuss it. There were a few short discussions, after which the subject festered. No one was willing to talk about it openly because one woman was in favor of trying it and her husband was the most conservative person in the group. Instead, it was the major "bed talk" subject for several months, after which the group disintegrated (Alam, 1974). In another group, one couple was monogamous whereas the other members were intimate friends. The group broke up because the monogamous couple was so threatened by the nonmonogamous others.

Singles are at a real disadvantage in a couple oriented group unless there is a bisexual pattern in the group as well. Often, even bisexual groups freeze out singles if there are strong primary relationship ties among most group members and the singles do not wish to be involved in a primary relationship. Singles involved in primary relationships have no such problem. Even in groups without couples initially, pairing tends to occur unless the group makes a conscious effort to prohibit or at least inhibit the formation of couples.

Social nudity is a rather common aspect of complex living groups, which serves to defuse the sexual overtones of the multi-adult household. The generally held view of nudity as a form of depravity, or, at the very least, of sexual titillation is an irrational rationalization. It is the other way around. The use of clothing and partial nudity is much more arousing than nudity. Those who have visited nudist camps or beaches will testify that nothing could be less erotic than a bunch of naked people playing canasta or sunbathing. The symbolic stripping away of facades in the act of taking off one's clothes has been used effectively in encounter and sensitivity groups; and it has even more meaning in a closed group in which there is sincere interest in furthering growth among intimate friends and in minimizing flirting and posturing as unnecessary distractions.

There seems to be pretty general agreement that the children are the real winners in complex living groups, perhaps because they reap so many more benefits without the attendent hassles that adults must invariably work through. Adult members already have highly structured lives and must work out mutually acceptable accommodations, whereas the children are relatively unstructured and can adapt quickly to the enriched environment. Perhaps the single most important aspect of the socialization of children in a complex living group is the availability of multiple adult models, each of whom has a different approach to life, different competencies, and different ways of relating to others. One of the difficulties of childhood for children who grow up in unorthodox homes is the discrepancy between the parental world view and that of the other adults in the environment. A multidimensional view right in the home is vastly reassuring to the child. The child is also likely to develop many more skills in a situation in which there are several teachers around, not just dad and mom. Because the parents have plenty of surrogates, parental hovering also relaxes in most cases, giving the child more freedom to be his or herself. In one complex living group, one family finally left the group because the father was unable to stop hovering over his daughter, overprotecting her, and thereby causing dissension among the rest of the group.

In a complex living group, sexual taboos are usually relaxed enough to be significant for the children. Children are not so completely shielded from awareness of adult sexuality. Social nudity is desensitizing for them as well as for the adults. Growing up among a variety of caring, sharing adults is especially important, because in many nuclear families there is a withdrawal from holding, touching, and caressing between mothers and sons and between fathers and children of both sexes at about age eleven, or with the onset of puberty. The children may be as withdrawing as the parents at this stage in their lives; but in any event, there is a strong sense of withdrawing with overtones of fear, insecurity, worry about the incest taboo, and often also with a sense of loss of love and affection. In a group household there are nonparents who can sometimes be less inhibited than parents about continuing the nonverbal and physical expression and reassurance of caring that the child has always received up until the onset of puberty. This is an important factor in keeping the channels of communication open between adults and children.

The complex living group is also a more exciting place to live for children. It generally involves a larger house, more children living in the house, and more things to do, because there always seems to be a lot going on in such a group. Children generally do better in school and improve in social adjustment (L & J Constantine, 1973). If the group decides to break up, the children are usually the most vocal in favor of staying together.

In some groups, the transition from childhood to personhood

takes place at a much younger age than in traditional families. The child is regarded as a junior partner rather than a subject species and allowed to participate at the level of his or her capabilities in work, decision-making, and play. It seems as though the shift in adult perspective from traditional family to sharing group breaks up the roles of family members sufficiently to allow the child gradually to become a group member, assuming responsibilities and participating in authority as he is able. In some groups this shift begins before the child is old enough to go to kindergarten (Berger, Hackett & Miller, 1972).

Complex living groups that grow out of intimate groups and networks tend to replicate the wide age range in intimate groups rather than to involve age peers, as communes often do. Thus they can draw on a variety of life experiences and world views. This is both more stimulating generally and very valuable in problem-solving situations. One of the real handicaps of age-peer groups has been their common level of experience and frequently common point of view, which inhibits problem-solving because everybody brings the same background to the situation. The mixing of married and single individuals serves a similar purpose in providing different points of view along another vector, as does the inclusion of homosexual or bisexual members with respect to yet another vector.

With the addition of each of these viewpoints, based on age, marital status, or sexual preference, the world view of the group is enlarged; and while the level of internal conflict may increase, the growth rate is accelerated for everyone at the same time. Conflict is an integral part of group living and ground rules are particularly important. The group must develop a decision-making structure and its own norms, standards and activities, or informal structure for getting things done. One can quickly gauge the relative success of a group by asking how old the group is, and then by observing the degree to which they feel compelled to invoke formal structure and rules in everyday living. A group that has been in existence for six months or more should only have to resort to the formal rules on infrequent occasions.

Small groups normally develop informal structure rather

quickly and soon dispense with the cumbersome joint decision structure (usually consensus) through the mechanism of delegating authority to various group members to handle certain types of decisions. If the person in charge of transportation, for example, has a decision to make with which she feels uncomfortable, she will probably confer with someone else about it, and if necessary, will carry the decision back to the group as a whole to decide. In this manner, decision authority is split up among group members according to their interests and abilities, and the time spent in "committee as a whole" hashing out decisions is cut to a minimum. This modus operandi can be called trust. In organization theory, it is called differentiation of function; and it occurs at the point at which it gets too difficult to work all day and then sit up half the night reviewing the day, approving decisions, and making decisions for the next day. Without trust there can be no delegation of authority and responsibility.

In an earlier chapter we talked about the need for structure in a complex living group. It is worth repeating that "do your own thing" is not conducive to the continued existence of any group. On the other hand, structure need not mean regimentation. Just as in a research or executive occupation there is vast time flexibility, as long as the deadline is met and standards of excellence are maintained, so in a complex living group is it possible to maintain a great deal of flexibility in task achievement as long as the task is completed satisfactorily and on time. Naturally some tasks provide less leeway than others, but in general it is usually possible to distribute tasks in order to give each individual the kind of flexibility s/he desires. In one household, the shopping for groceries is rotated. One person prefers to shop for the week at one time, while another may make as many as three or four trips during the week. In that particular group, the shopper also plans the meals. The group has learned that one individual will invariably spend much more than anyone else if she shops alone, so they have a rule, to which she agreed, that either the group will accept the added cost without griping or send someone along with her to the market.

Some groups, especially those in which all the adults have full

time jobs outside the home, hire full time professional house-
keepers or housekeeper/cooks. The group mentioned in the
previous paragraph is one of these. In that group, the shopping
and meal planning tasks are retained, but in others the meals are
planned by the group but the shopping is done by the
housekeeper. Many young people have expressed wonder and
indignation at the thought of a complex living group in which
the chores are handled by a paid professional, seeing this as
"saddling" some other poor woman with the "woman's work."
This point of view ignores the fact that paid outside employment
for the housekeeper may be as important to her as their own
outside job is to them, and can hardly be classified as "exploita-
tion" at today's wages. A housekeeper/cook gets $8,000 + per
year, including a paid vacation and holidays off, Social Security,
hospitalization, and sick leave. Even in today's economy, this is
not a bad situation for someone without other saleable skills.

We can reasonably expect the number of multi- adult
households to show a gradual increase over the next ten years. If
"consenting adult" and/or multiple-adult marriage laws are
modified significantly during this decade, growth of such households might increase more dramatically; but in any event, the
total number of such households will not become a significant
portion of the total households in the nation before 1990. It is not
realistic to make projections beyond 1990 based on present data.
It is extremely safe to say, however, that there will be millions of
people living in traditional marriages and households at that
time. A dramatic shift in the society from dyadic marriage to
complex living groups does not seem at all likely in this century.
A shift for some segments of the population from traditional to
peer marriage is a much stronger possibility in the next fifteen
years.

13

The Impact of These Changes
on
Various Social Institutions

"The partnership form of marriage faces difficulties from outside forces such as the media as well as from the internal tendency of spouses to drift into more traditional sex roles" (Perrucci and Targ, 1974). In an interesting article, Susan Sutheim (1974) discusses the ways in which women's magazines have shifted ground to accommodate the needs of their advertisers respecting the image they project for women to follow since World War II. They have consistently denied that there is a sexual revolution going on: They claim that naturally young women will get married and will have children within marriage rather than outside of marriage, because the nuclear family is the focal point of the purchase of consumer goods. The economy and society might be seriously threatened if people were allowed to realize that we actually live in a pluralistic society *today;* and that alternatives to marriage into a traditional family setting are indeed possible.

The Census Bureau does not keep figures on cohabiting couples because "cohabiting couples are not an important consumer entity!" Marriage makes business, living together doesn't; so, according to Sutheim's quote from *McCall's*, "I need to find fixed and immutable aspects to the relationship of man and woman, and so I find them. I find them by refusing to accept a viable alternative to a stable family for the rearing of offspring." In other words, the business community deals with the threat posed by marriage alternatives by denying that they exist, or by redefining them into nonthreats. Cohabitation is redefined as a prelude to marriage rather than as an alternative to marriage, for example.

This threat to business is very real. Multiperson households, in particular, pose real threats to the producers of such basic consumer goods as household appliances, furniture, automobiles, and housing. Cohabitors are a threat for they do not buy many of the goods and services that couples are expected to buy because they are less likely to feel the sense of permanence that is a prerequisite for purchasing items on time, such as home furnishings, life insurance, automobiles, and the like. They are more likely to restrict purchases to items that are personally owned and easy to divide if they should split up. Even trios and tetrads, which we regard as the most likely of the emerging new groupings, have an impact on basic consumer goods industries. On the other hand, the emerging complex living groups should add to the sales of top-of-the-line and luxury items because of their increased discretionary buying power. Expenses are reduced drastically in most complex living groups, and at least some of the excess finds its way into luxury purchases.

As more upper-middle class individuals reveal their pluralistic lifestyles, the pluralistic revolution will be reflected in a redefinition of the underlying assumptions about what constitutes dysfunction and eufunction. Non-nuclear households that are now classified as "deviant" will be reclassified as different, but not deviant; and this will result in considerable changes in the mental health of our society as defined by the human service delivery systems. Since, as Birdwhistell noted (1974), the ideal nuclear family is used as the model of normalcy not only in science, art, and the media, but also by our legal, social, psychiatric, and religious experts, we are in the position of having all the agencies designed to assist those in trouble accept as ideal the very condition which occasioned the difficulty, so that the very devices for ameliorating social pathology contribute to it instead. Thus by simply redefining normalcy to include the many already existing non-nuclear family forms, we will eliminate, by a stroke of the pen, a major part of the so-called dysfunctional, or deviant (or sick) behavior.

Having done so, we will discover a "multiplier effect," because knowing that they will no longer be labeled deviant will free many more people to reveal their non-nuclear households. This will result in a re-appraisal of the actual extent of pluralistic lifestyles, which are currently either underestimated or denied altogether by being lumped into categories that hide them in census and other statistical measures. Once the market is revealed to be significant, business will quickly adapt to it. We can see this happening today in two markets, for example, education and housing.

In education, the pluralistic revolution has had tremendous impact in a few short years. Loco parentis has all but disappeared from most public campuses, and has suffered serious inroads on most private campuses. A recent study by the American College Health Association indicates that 90 per cent of all North American colleges and universities now offer formal or informal learning opportunities concerning human sexuality, and that about 20 per cent are providing formal family planning, and contraceptive information and services. As recently as 1966 only 4 per cent of these services prescribed birth control pills for unmarried students. In addition to the 20 per cent now providing these services, 32 per cent refer the students to such services elsewhere (Chronicle of Higher Education, 1975).

The move to co-ed dorms and the fact that administrations allow increasing numbers of students to live off campus have also grown to become majority expectations. Colleges that were willing to expel a student for a single act of intercourse ten years ago condone cohabitation in the dorms today. The sex orgies predicted by outraged parents and legislators never occurred, of course, because the same kind of exogamy occurs in the dorm as in intimate groups and networks, that is, people tend not to become intimate with someone with whom they live, not because of a kind of incest taboo, but because of the potential difficulties that could result if the relationship breaks up and they are unable to withdraw from the scene. College dorms are rampant with rumors and intrigue, and few couples are brave enough to face this on their own floor and perhaps in their own dorm. Intimacy patterns are likely to reflect this desire to avoid potential problems. If a romance does develop, the two are likely to move off campus, or one switches to another dorm as a means of protecting the relationship and the individuals involved from the environment. This is precisely why intimate groups and networks flourish. Each participant can withdraw from involvement at will because the participants do not live together; thus each is protected from emotional overload and from the potential unpleasantness of having to stay together after the relationship cools.

But this is not the only impact of the pluralistic revolution on education. Education as an industry will undergo further modification as a result of the slowing of the birth rate. Public schools are already feeling the impact of the free school movement, which is often associated with complex living groups. As we have already mentioned, these groups are financially able to shift their children to private schools or to tutors, and they are able to provide their members as well as their children with a wider choice of higher education opportunities. Education has been slow to grasp the opportunity to meet the needs of adult women who want to enter the job market. The current adult education offerings are generally pablum courses; and in regular courses, adults are less likely to stand still for many of the things professors can get away with in classes of twenty year olds. As the youth enrollments drop, the colleges can be expected to pay considerably more attention to this new group of clients. The pluralistic revolution's growing impact on housing is evident also.

The housing market has already realigned itself to take advantage of a couple of segments of the non-nuclear market. Builders are well aware that the pluralistic revolution is here, and they have responded with specialized housing for singles and for childless couples. They have found this to be a very lucrative market. Apartment complexes for singles have many amenities not found in other housing, such as indoor and outdoor pools, saunas, recreation rooms, squash courts, other recreation areas, and often even a social director. This is a plastic turn-off for many people, but not for others; and landlords have found that they can arrange their apartments in a way that caters to those who want such things without offending those who do not. Similar apartment complexes are widely available for childless couples, a natural outgrowth of the success with singles-only apartments.

As the market for other kinds of relationships becomes defined, you can rest assured that builders will be quick to respond to the need. Up until now, most complex living groups have either custom built or reworked existing housing to their special needs. There has been little agreement on ideal designs for such groups because group needs and desires have differed drastically. Some have bought large homes or estates and provided each member with a private room while sharing all other space in common. Some groups have shared rooms but have designated a private space for each member according to his/her desires. Some have only a single privacy room where a member can go to be alone for a while. At the other extreme, some groups have separate complete apartments for each couple or family in the group plus shared common space. In some instances this has taken the form of a jointly owned apartment complex; others occupy a group of houses in a jointly owned setting. Some older groups own homes in several states or countries.

The personal and economic sharing that we have discussed with respect to complex living groups extends to intimate groups and networks too, although on a lesser scale. Many two-couple groups buy second homes together at the shore or in the mountains, or jointly own a boat or some other luxury purchase. Larger groups often jointly purchase seldom used equipment and other amenities, such as a truck or a mobile home for vacations, investment property, or a farm for vacations and depreciation.

It is reasonable to assume that the formation of both intimate friendship groups and complex living groups will result in increased geographic stability for many people, particularly if economic sharing is involved. In dual-career families we can see some evidence of a trend in this direction; and in three and four person groups it is even more pronounced. With several people bringing in paychecks, no one person is at the mercy of a corporate decision to move every few years. Such groups can decide where they want to live and stay there as long as they wish, without running the risk of subjecting the family to a lowered standard of living because one person refused a corporate move to a new location. This should ultimately result in greater political leverage at the local level for people who in many cases have been effectively disenfranchised because of their frequent moves.

A group of academic, professional, creative, and managerial people who are property owners, respected community leaders, and politically active can be a very positive influence in the community. As such groups become more visible, other people are more likely to consider emulating them; for in our society, nothing succeeds like success, and the enhanced economic clout of such groups will not long be lost on others. The legitimization of such groups will probably be achieved via the courts rather than through legislation, although the way may be indirectly opened by legislation. A direct challenge on Constitutional grounds of the right of the community to prevent free association will probably be successfully fought within the next ten years by a complex living group.

The focus of this book has been on CONSCIOUS CHOICE. Recognizing full well that many individuals will continue to make the kind of choice most people have made in the past, we have endeavored to raise critical issues that might help make the process a deliberate one, rather than one that simply seems to happen because everyone expects it to happen. We believe that much of the unhappiness that occurs in interpersonal relationships, including primary relationships, occurs because the *actuality* never equals the *anticipation*. The reason for this discrepancy is that *we do not fantasize the problems that will occur in the relationship, only the pleasures.* This is true of all of the relationship alternatives we have discussed, from the least to the most complex. Even when we talk to others who have experienced the kind of relationship in which we are interested, they are unable to tell us about the problems (even assuming we would listen) because people tend to remember pleasant things more easily than painful things.

The mass media may be in part responsible for fostering unrealistic anticipations with respect to relationships. On television, problems are never presented that cannot be dealt with in either 21 or 42 minutes, the programming time in 30 and 60 minute TV shows. The distortion that must result takes the form of truncating problem solutions, or dealing with trivial problems, or both. Oddly enough, the message thus produced contains a double whammy. It reduces credibility, but at the same time the subliminal message is that the problems aren't really all that tough. This subtle message is 180 degrees out of phase with reality. If the problems weren't tough, we wouldn't see one out of three of the couples who separate or divorce do so within the first year of marriage.

The credibility issue is becoming more and more a factor in all areas of our society. The fact of the matter is that faster communication and less credibility are two sides of the same coin. You can't have one without the other. In previous generations, say that of my great-grandfather and my great great-grandfather, there was little change in the world as both saw it. Communication between father and son was much easier because each had essentially the same world view. Their contemporaries heard about vital changes in the world very slowly. The process of assimilating change was accordingly a less threatening process because changes filtered through the social fabric at an almost imperceptible rate.

Today the changes are occurring so rapidly that the process of assimilation cannot possibly keep up. By the time we begin to get used to one new shift, two succeeding ones have occurred. There are those who are now predicting that the accelerating rate of change will soon begin to slow down. Evidence for such a slow down is lacking, however, and it appears more likely that people will learn to adapt to change faster because the instantaneous means of communication are not going to go away. Those who have grown up in an era of TV satellites that bring us live coverage of events in China as easily as those across the street—that show us men walking on the moon—are paradoxically the most susceptible to disbelief. Ghetto children interviewed after the moon walk refused to believe that what they saw on television was real. They maintained that they had been watching "made-up" science fiction and not reality.

We hope that this book will help counteract some of the sense of nonreality some people have about the alternative lifestyles available to the individual today. We have made every effort to stay within the bounds of what we know is happening right now, on the assumption that the more we know about what is happening today, the better equipped we will be to make choices about tomorrow.

Bibliography

PART I

MACKLIN, E. D. "Comparison of Parent and Student Attitudes Toward Non-marital Cohabitation." Paper presented at NCFR Annual Meeting, St. Louis, October 1974.

CHAPTER 1

BERNE, E. *Games People Play.* New York: Grove Press, 1964.

BLOOD, R. O. "The Husband-Wife Relationship." *The Employed Mother in America.* Ed. F. I. Nye and L. W. Hoffman. Chicago: Rand McNally, 1963.

BOHANNAN, P. *Social Anthropology.* New York, Holt, 1963.

CAPLOW, THEODORE. *Two Against One.* Englewood Cliffs, N.J.: Prentice-Hall, 1968.

CUBER, JOHN F. "Alternate Models from the Perspective of Sociology." *The Family in Search of a Future.* Ed. Herbert A. Otto. New York: Appleton, Century, Crofts, 1970.

DAHRENDORF, R. "Out of Utopia: Toward a Reorientation of Sociological Analysis." *American Journal of Sociology*, 64, No. 2 (1958), 115–27.

DOUVAN, ELIZABETH. "Employment and the Adolescent." *The Employed Mother in America.* Ed. F. I. Nye and L. W. Hoffman. Chicago: Rand McNally, 1963.

DUNCAN, S. "Nonverbal Communication." *Psychological Bulletin,* LXII (1969), pp. 127–132.

GOODE, W. J. *World Revolution and Family Patterns.* New York: Free Press, 1963.

HALEY, J. *Strategies of Psychotherapy.* New York: Grune & Stratton, 1963.

HARRIS, M. *The Rise of Anthropological Theory: A History of Theories of Culture.* New York: Crowell, 1968.

HENLEY, N. M. "Power, Sex, and Nonverbal Communication." *Doing Unto Others.* Ed. Zick Rubin. Englewood Cliffs, N.J.: Prentice-Hall Spectrum, 1974.

KINSEY, ALFRED C., W. B. POMEROY, C. E. MARTIN and P. H. GEBHARD. *Sexual Behavior in the Human Female.* Philadelphia: W. B. Saunders Company, 1953.

KUHN, T. *The Structure of Scientific Revolutions.* Chicago: University of Chicago Press, 1962.

LAING, R. D. *The Politics of the Family.* New York: Random House, 1971.

LASLETT, BARBARA. "The Family as a Public and Private Institution: A Historical Perspective." *Journal of Marriage and the Family,* 35, No. 3 (August 1973).

MEAD, MARGARET. Narrator of "Family: Life Styles of the Future." Film distributed by University of California Extension Media Center, 1968.

MOORE, B. M. JR. "Thoughts on the Future of the Family." *Political Power and Social Theory.* Cambridge, Mass.: Harvard University Press, 1958. (Cited in *The Sociological Perspective.* Ed. S. G. McNall. Boston: Little Brown, 1968, pp. 407–17.)

NOORDHOEK, J. A. and YRSA SMITH. *Married Women, Family, and Work.* Vol. II: *Effects on the Family.* Copenhagen: Teknisk Forlag, 1972.

NYE, F. I. and L. W. HOFFMAN. *The Employed Mother in America.* Chicago: Rand McNally, 1963.

PARSONS, TALCOTT. *The Social System.* Glencoe, Ill.: Free Press, 1951.

RAMEY, JAMES W. "Emerging Patterns of Innovation in Marriage." *The Family Coordinator,* 21, No. 4, October 1972a.

RAMEY, JAMES W. "Superfamily: The Competitive Edge in the 70's?" Keynote address, Groves Conference on Marriage and the Family. Dallas, May 1972b.

RAMEY, JAMES W. *Almost Group Marriage.* Mimeograph. New York: CSILS, 1973.

RYDER, N. B. and C. F. WESTOFF. "Fertility Planning Status: United States, 1965." *Demography*, VI (1969), 435-44.

SKOLNICK, ARLENE. *The Intimate Environment.* Boston: Little Brown, 1973.

SLATER, P. E. "Some Social Consequences of Temporary Systems." *The Temporary Society.* Ed. W. G. Bennis and P. E. Slater. New York: Harper and Row, 1968.

SPIEGEL, J. *Transactions: The Interplay between Individual, Family and Society.* New York: Science House, 1971.

SULLEROT, EVELYNE. *Women, Society and Change.* New York: McGraw-Hill, 1971.

TAVRIS, CAROL and TOBY JAYARATNE. "What 120,000 Young Women Can Tell You About Sex, Motherhood, Menstruation, Housework— and Men." *Redbook*, 140, No. 3 (1973), 67-69.

UDRY, J. R. *The Social Context of Marriage.* 3rd ed. Philadelphia: Lippincott, 1974.

CHAPTER 2

COGSWELL, B. E. and M. B. SUSSMAN. "Changing Family and Marriage Forms." *Family Coordinator*, 21, No. 4 (1972), pp. 505-516.

CONSTANTINE, L. L. and J. M. *Group Marriage.* New York: Macmillan, 1973.

CUBER, J. F. and P. B. HAROFF. *Sex and the Significant Americans.* Baltimore: Penguin, 1966.

DODSON, BETTY. *Liberating Masturbation.* New York: Bodysex Designs, 1974.

ETZIONI, AMITAI. "The Next Crisis—The End of the Family?" *Human Behavior*, August 1974, pp. 10-11.

FRANCOEUR, R. T. and A. K. "Hot and Cool Sex: Fidelity in Marriage." *Renovating Marriage.* Ed. R. W. Libby and R. N. Whitehurst, Danville, Calif.: Consensus, 1973.

GEBHARD, PAUL. Quoted by Morton Hunt. *The Affair.* New York: World, 1969.

HARRIS, DENAH. Personal communication, 1960.

KINSEY, ALFRED C., Wardell Pomeroy and Clyde Martin. *Sexual Behavior in the Human Male.* Philadelphia: Saunders, 1948.

KINSEY, ALFRED C. et al. 1953 ibid.

KNAPP, J. J. "An Exploratory Study of Seventeen Personal Growth Oriented Sexually Open Marriages." *Family Coordinator*, 24, No. 4, 1975.

MACKLIN, E. D. *Unmarried Heterosexual Cohabitation on the University Campus.* Unpublished manuscript. Cornell University, Ithaca, N.Y., 1974.

PETERMAN, DAN. "Towards Interpersonal Fulfillment in an Eupsychian Culture." *Journal of Humanistic Psychology.* Spring 1972, as cited in *Hot and Cool Sex.* A. K. and R. T. Francoeur. New York: Harcourt Brace Jovanovich, 1974, p. 44.

RAMEY, JAMES W. "Communes, Group Marriage, and the Upper Middle Class." *Journal of Marriage and the Family*, 34, No. 4 (1972c), 647–55.

———. "Emerging Patterns of Innovation in Marriage." *Family Coordinator,* 21, No. 4 (1972a).

———. "Intimate Groups and Networks: Frequent Consequence of Sexually Open Marriage." *Family Coordinator*, 24, No. 4 (1975a).

SUSSMAN, M. B. and M. GOLD. "Personal Marriage Contracts: Old Wine in New Bottles." Cleveland: Institute on the Family and Bureaucratic Society, 1974.

VEEVERS, J. E. "The Child-Free Alternative: Rejection of the Motherhood Mystique." *Women in Canada.* Ed. M. Stephenson. Toronto: New Press, 1973.

WATTS, ALAN. *Nature, Man and Woman.* New York: Random House, 1970.

WHITEHURST, R. N. "Sex-Role Equality and Changing Meanings in Cohabitation." Paper delivered at NCFR annual meeting. St. Louis, 1974.

CHAPTER 3

COLTON, HELEN. *Sex After the Sexual Revolution.* As quoted in *Buffalo Courier-Express* interview, March 10, 1974.

CONSTANTINE, L. L. and J. M. *Group Marriage.* New York: Macmillan, 1973.

COOLEY, C. H. *Social Organization: A Study of the Larger Mind.* New York: Schocken Books, 1962.

ETZIONI, AMITAI. "The Next Crisis—The End of the Family?" *Human Behavior,* August 1974.

KANTER, R. B. *Commitment and Community.* Cambridge, Mass.: Harvard Univ. Press, 1972.

KNAPP, JACQUELYN J. "Co-Marital Sex and Marriage Counseling." Diss., University of Florida, Gainsville, 1974.

RAMEY, JAMES W. "Communes, Group Marriage, and the Upper Middle Class."

RAMEY, JAMES W. "Intimate Groups and Networks: Frequent Consequence of Sexually Open Marriage." *Family Coordinator*, 24, No. 4 (1975a).

STOLLER, F. H. "The Intimate Network of Families as a New Structure." *The Family in Search of a Future*. Ed. H. A. Otto. New York: Appleton, Century, Crofts, 1970, pp. 145–159.

SULLIVAN, H. S. *Conceptions in Modern Psychiatry*. Washington, D.C.: Wm Allison White Psychiatric Foundation, 1947.

TIGER, LIONEL. *Men in Groups*. New York: Random House, 1970.

TIGER, LIONEL and ROBIN FOX. *The Imperial Animal*. New York: Holt, Rinehart and Winston, 1971.

WEISS, R. S. "The Provisions of Social Relationships," Zick Rubin, ed. *Doing Unto Others*. Ed. Zick Rubin. Englewood Cliffs, N.J.: Prentice-Hall Spectrum, 1974.

CHAPTER 4

BERGER, B., B. M. HACKETT and R. M. MILLER. "Child-rearing Practices in the Communal Family." Unpublished progress report to National Institute of Mental Health, 1972. Quoted in Skolnick, Arlene. *The Intimate Environment*. Boston: Little Brown, 1973, pp. 425–26.

EDMISTON, SUSAN. "Boys will Be Boys, Girls will be Girls, or will They?" *New York Times Book Review*, April 13, 1975, p. 3.

HOBBS, E. C. "An Alternative Model from a Theological Perspective." *The Family in Search of a Future*. Ed. H. A. Otto. New York: Appleton, Century, Crofts, 1970.

KOHLBERG, L. and D. Z. ULLIAN. Chapter in Ed. R. C. Friedman, R. M. Richart and R. L. Vande Wiele, *Sex Differences in Behavior*. New York: Wiley, 1975.

MACCOBY, E. E. and C. N. JACKLIN. *Psychology of Sex Differences*. Stanford: Stanford U. Press, 1975.

PINEO, P. C. "Disenchantment in the Later Years of Marriage." *Marriage and Family Living*, 23 (1961), pp. 3–11.

RAMEY, JAMES W. "Getting More Mileage from Your Marriage." Christian Marriage Conference presentation, New York, 1960.

RAMEY, JAMES W. "Emerging Patterns of Innovation in Marriage." *The Family Coordinator*, 21, No. 4, Otober 1972a.

SKOLNICK, ARLENE. *The Intimate Environment.* Boston: Little Brown, 1973.

SPEER, D. C. "Family Systems: Morphostatis and Morphogenesis, or Is Homeostatis Enough?" *Family Process,* 9 (September 1970), 259–78.

WIENER, N. *Cybernetics, Control and Communication in the Animal and the Machine.* New York: Wiley, 1948.

————. *The Human Use of Human Beings: Cybernetics and Society.* Boston: Houghton Mifflin, 1950.

CHAPTER 5

CAIRD, MONA. Essays on the acceptance of trial marriage, in Karl Pearson, *Ethics of Free Thought,* 1890, as reported in R. T. Francoeur, *Eve's New Rib.* New York: Dell, 1972, p. 61.

CUBER, J. F. "Alternate Models from the Perspective of Sociology." *The Family in Search of a Future.* Ed. Herbert A. Otto. New York: Appleton-Century-Crofts, 1970.

DAVIDS, LEO. "New Family Norms." *The Future of Sexual Relations.* Ed. R. T. and A. K. Francoeur. Englewood Cliffs, N.J.: Prentice-Hall Spectrum, 1974.

FRANCOEUR, R. T. *Eve's New Rib.* New York: Dell, 1972, p. 76.

HOBBS, E. C. "An Alternative Model from a Theological Perspective." *The Family in Search of a Future.* Ed. H. A. Otto. New York: Appleton, Century, Crofts, 1970.

KELLER, SUZANNE. "Does the Family Have a Future?" *Journal of Comparative Family Studies,* Spring 1971, pp. 1–14.

LINDSEY, B. B. and W. EVANS. *The Companionate Marriage.* Garden City, N.Y.: Garden City Publishing Company, 1929.

MAZUR, R. *The New Intimacy.* Boston: Beacon, 1973, p. 28.

MEAD, MARGARET. "Marriage in Two Steps." In Otto, H. A. ed. *The Family in Search of a Future* (New York: Appleton, Century, Crofts, 1970), pp. 75–84.

SPREY, JETSE. "On the Institutionalization of Sexuality." *Journal of Marriage and the Family,* 31, No. 3 (1969), 432–41.

PART II

CHAPTER 6

Anon. IDEAS, *Newsweek*, (11/5/73), p. 82.

Berger, M. E. "Trial Marriage: Harnessing the Trend Constructively." *Family Coordinator*, 20, No. 1 (1971), 38–43.

Birdwhistell, Ray. Personal communication to the author from Birdwhistell, 1967.

Coleman, J. S. ed. *Youth: Transition to Adulthood.* Chicago: U. of Chicago Press, 1974.

Comfort, Alex. "Sexuality in a Zero Growth Society." *Center Report*, Santa Barbara: Center for the Study of Democratic Institutions, December 1972.

Constantine, L. L. and J. M. "Where Is Marriage Going?" *The Futurist*, 4, No. 2 (1970), p. 46.

de Beauvoir, S. *The Second Sex.* New York: Alfred P. Knopf, 1953.

Feldman, H. "The Effects of Children on the Family." *Family Issues of Employed Women in Europe and America.* Ed. A. Michel. Leiden, The Netherlands: Brill, 1971.

Goodrich, W., R. G. Ryder and H. L. Raush. "Patterns of Newlywed Marriage." *Journal of Marriage and the Family*, 30, No. 2 (1968), 383–91.

Hoffman, L. W. and F. I. Nye. *Working Mothers.* San Francisco: Jossey-Bass, 1974.

Macklin, E. D. "Cohabitation in College: Going Very Steady." *Psychology Today*, 8, No. 6 (1974), 53–59.

O'Neill, Nena and George. *Open Marriage.* New York: Evans, 1972.

Otto, H. A. *The Family Cluster.* Beverly Hills: Holistic Press, 1971.

Rimmer, R. H. *Proposition 31*, New York: New American Library, 1968.

Roy, Rustum and Della. *Honest Sex*, New York: New American Library, 1968.

U.S. News and World Report surveys on family size in *Hot and Cool Sex.* A. K. and R. T. Francoeur. New York: Harcourt Brace Jovanovich, 1974, p. 67.

CHAPTER 7

FOOTE, NELSON. "Matching of Husband and Wife in Phases of Development." *Sourcebook in Marriage and the Family*, Ed. M. B. Sussman. 2nd ed. Boston: Houghton Mifflin, 1963, pp. 17-19.

FRANCOEUR, R. T. and A. K. "Hot and Cool Sex: Fidelity in Marriage."

HEINLEIN, R. A. *Stranger in a Strange Land.* New York: Berkley, 1961.

MASTERS, W. H. and V. E. JOHNSON. *Human Sexual Response.* Boston: Little Brown, 1966.

MEAD, MARGARET. *The Anatomy of Love.* A. M. Krich. New York: Dell, 1960.

MYERS, LONNY. "Marriage, Honesty and Personal Growth." *Renovating Marriage.* Ed. R. W. Libby and R. N. Whitehurst. Danville, Calif.: Consensus, 1973.

ROLLINS, B. C. and H. FELDMAN. "Marital Satisfaction over the Family Life Cycle." *Journal of Marriage and the Family*, 32, No. 1 (1970), 20-8.

ROY, RUSTUM and DELLA. "Is Monogamy Outdated?" in *Renovating Marriage*, R. W. Libby and R. N. Whitehurst, eds. Danville, Calif.: Consensus Publishers, 1973, pp. 59-73.

SMITH, J. R. and L. G. *Beyond Monogamy.* Baltimore: Johns Hopkins U. Press, 1974.

SMITH, LYNN, and JAY SMITH. *Consenting Adults*, unpublished manuscript, 1975.

CHAPTER 8

CONSTANTINE, L. L. and J. M. *Group Marriage.* New York: Macmillan, 1973.

CUBER, J. F. and P. B. Haroff. *Sex and the Significant Americans.* Baltimore: Penguin, 1966.

CHAPTER 9

GOLDSTEIN, LEE. *Communes, Law and Commonsense.* Boston: New Community Projects, 1974.

GRONSETH, ERIK. "Work Sharing Families." *Twelfth International Seminar on Family Research.* Moscow, April 17–23, 1972.

MELVILLE, KEITH. *Communes in the Counter Culture.* New York: Morrow, 1972.

RAMEY, JAMES W. "Communes, Group Marriage, and the Upper Middle Class."

ROSSI, ALICE. "A Good Woman Is Hard to Find." *Marriage and the Family.* Ed. C. C. Perrucci and D. B. Targ. New York: McKay, 1974.

WEISBERG, D. K. "Alternative Family Structures and the Law." *Family Coordinator,* 24, No. 4 (October 1975).

CHAPTER 10

DANZIGER, CARL, and MATHEW GREENWALD. *Alternatives: A Look at Unmarried Couples and Communes.* New York: Institute of Life Insurance, 1973.

LINDEMANN, CONSTANCE. *Birth Control and Unmarried Young Women.* New York: Springer, 1975.

RAMEY, JAMES W. "Structure and Dynamics of Intimate Networks." *The Next 25 Years: Crisis and Opportunity.* Washington, D.C.: World Future Society, 1975b.

RAMEY, James W. "Viewing Client Life Styles as Dysfunctional or Eufunctional." Paper presented at International Conference on Gender Role Equality, Dubrovnik, Yugoslavia, June 1975.

U.S. News and World Report (1/3/1972).

CHAPTER 11

CONSTANTINE, L. L. and J. M. Plenary session, Future Families of the World Conference, April, 1975, U. of Maryland.

CONSTANTINE, L. L. and J. M. "Where Is Marriage Going?" *The Futurist,* 4, No. 2 (1970), p. 46.

LYNES, RUSSELL. *A Surfeit of Honey.* New York: Harper, 1953.

MACKLIN, E. D. *Unmarried Heterosexual Cohabitation on the University Campus.* Unpublished manuscript. Cornell University, Ithaca, N.Y., 1974.

MAZUR, RONALD. *The New Intimacy.* Boston: Beacon, 1973.

OTTO, H. A. *The Family Cluster.* Beverly Hills: Holistic, 1971.

Perrucci, C. C. and D. B. Targ. *Marriage and the Family*. New York: McKay, 1974.

Ramey, James W. "Intimate Groups and Networks: Frequent Consequence of Sexually Open Marriage." *Family Coordinator*, 24, No. 4 (1975a).

Stoller, F. H. "The Intimate Network of Families as a New Structure." *The Family in Search of a Future*. Ed. H. A. Otto. New York: Appleton, Century, Crofts, 1970, pp. 145–59.

Udry, J. R. *The Social Context of Marriage*. 3rd ed. Philadelphia: Lippincott, 1974.

CHAPTER 12

Alam, S. F. "Middle Class Communes: A Case Study and Research Proposal." Paper presented at the annual meeting, National Council on Family Relations. St. Louis, October 24, 1974.

Berger, B., B. M. Hackett, and R. M. Miller. "Child-rearing Practices in the Communal Family." Unpublished progress report to the National Institute of Mental Health, 1972. Quoted in Skolnick, Arlene. *The Intimate Environment*. Boston: Little Brown, 1973, pp. 425–26.

Constantine, L. L. and J. M. *Group Marriage*. New York: Macmillan, 1973.

Slater, Philip. *Earthwalk*. New York: Doubleday, 1974.

CHAPTER 13

Anon. "Courses in Sexuality Gaining Ground." *Chronicle of Higher Education*, March 3, 1975, p. 6.

Birdwhistell, Ray. "The Idealized Model of the American Family." *Sourcebook in Marriage and the Family*. Ed. M. B. Sussman. 4th ed., Boston: Houghton Mifflin, 1974.

Perrucci, C. C. and D. B. Targ. *Marriage and the Family*. New York: McKay, 1974.

Sutheim, Susan. "The Subversion of Betty Crocker." *Marriage and the Family*. C. C. Perrucci and D. B. Targ. New York: McKay, 1974, pp. 292–93.